LIFE IN
RUSSIA TODAY

JACK MILLER

LIFE IN

RUSSIA TODAY

B. T. BATSFORD LTD
LONDON
G. P. PUTNAM'S SONS
NEW YORK

B. T. BATSFORD LTD
4 Fitzhardinge St., Portman Square, London W1

G. P. PUTNAM'S SONS
200 Madison Ave., New York, NY 10016

First published 1969 Copyright © J. Miller 1969

Printed and bound in Great Britain by
Jarrold and Sons Ltd, London & Norwich
Set in 11pt Monotype Imprint

7134 1554 1

ACKNOWLEDGMENT

The author and publishers would like to thank the following for the illustrations appearing in this book: Bild am Sonntag for pages 54, 76 and 77; Camera Press for pages 115, 133, 144, 157 and 158; Foto-khronika, Tass for pages 7 and 9; Henri Cartier-Bresson and Magnum Photos Inc. for page 39; John Massey Stewart for pages 4, 29, 31, 63, 81, 87, 89, 108, 143 and 183; Dr Katz for pages 32, 61, 67, 83 and 181; Keystone Press Agency for pages 35 and 44; Novosti Press Agency for pages 5, 19, 20, 36, 48, 71, 75, 90, 92, 97, 99, 101, 117, 119, 145, 147, 161, 164, 167, 174, 176 and 177 and *Life* Magazine for pages 58, 59, 93, 138 and 149.

CONTENTS

PREFACE

Most of the information in this book is personal. It comes from my own experience and observation of life in the USSR, discussions with many Soviet citizens, recent émigrés and foreign visitors, and from kind permission to read about 500 individual accounts collected over the past few years. For access to the last source I am greatly indebted to Dr Max Ralis. I am also particularly grateful to Mr Leonid Vladimirov who commented in critical detail on the book while it was being written. I am further indebted to Mr Vladimorov, and to Mr Rene Beermann, Mr Roger Clarke and other academic colleagues, for information on particular points. None of these friends is responsible for any errors of fact, form of presentation or opinion. For helpful patience in publishing I must thank Mr Peter Kemmis Betty of Batsfords, and in typing—Miss Eleanor Robertson and Miss Jean Fyfe.

I expected the main difficulty in writing this book to be inadequate information on Soviet life at the present time, but both personal and written sources have turned out to be fuller than anticipated. The chief difficulty has been one which must be present in depicting any country or period: life is rich and words on paper are poor.

In keeping with other books in the series, footnote references to the published sources are not included.

Mistakes of fact and disputed estimates are inevitable in a book on this subject. I shall be grateful to anybody kind enough to point them out and for any more general criticisms and suggestions.

Glasgow, August 1968   J.M.

A NOTE ON
ADMINISTRATIVE AREAS
AND LEVELS

The USSR consists of 15 Union Republics. The Russian Republic is by far the largest. It occupies nearly three-quarters of the whole area and contains over half the population. In addition to most of the Russian nation, the Russian Republic contains many small nations in 16 Autonomous Republics and various Autonomous Provinces and National Areas. The parts of the Russian Republic inhabited by Russians are divided into 55 provinces, most of which range in size from about the area of Holland to that of England, and in population from one to five million. In the undeveloped parts of Northern and Eastern Siberia the provinces are very much larger. The other two Union Republics inhabited by Slav nations are both in Europe: the Ukraine with 25 provinces and Byelorussia with six. Moldavia is a small Union Republic of mixed Slav and Latin culture between the Ukraine and Rumania.

Six of the other Union Republics are of Moslem population and situated in Asia. They are Azerbaijan in the Eastern Caucasus and five mainly desert or mountainous ones in Central Asia—Kazakhstan, which is divided into 15 provinces, Uzbekistan with nine provinces, and the small Union Republics of Kirgizia, Turkmenia and Tajikistan. Two very old small Christian nations, the Georgians and Armenians, have Union Republics on the Asiatic side of the Caucasus. Three small European nations have Union Republics on the Baltic—the Estonians, Latvians and Lithuanians.

The smaller Union Republics and most of the Autonomous Republics are roughly similar in area, population and economic importance to the provinces of the larger Union Republics, and there are about a dozen towns of similar economic and population weight. These republics, provinces and towns, which number about 150 altogether, form in practice the basic administrative units, although they are of very different formal constitutional importance.

The various levels of administration may be taken, in practice, as:

1   The USSR as a whole
2   The Union Republics of the Ukraine, Byelorussia, Uzbekistan and Kazakhstan

3 The 150 basic units noted above

4 About 1,000 towns of medium size

5 About 2,000 counties, each containing on the average about 25 giant state farms and collective farms

These five levels of administration, from the centre down to the counties, are the levels of the Communist Party hierarchy. (There is no distinct party organisation for the Russian republic because it is so large and its interests are regarded as in principle identical with those of the USSR.)

The Communist Party bureaus are the most powerful bodies at each level. These are the small executive groups supposedly appointed by the party committees, which are in turn supposed to be elected by delegates representing all the party members in the area. The bureaus are, however, appointed from the higher levels of party authority. Thus, the party bureau of a medium-sized town or a county is in effect appointed by the party bureau of the province in which it is located.

According to the constitution, power is exercised at all levels by the soviets, which are elected by all adult citizens. Thus the Supreme Soviet of the USSR is the product of a general election and it appoints the government (Council of Ministers). Each Union Republic and Autonomous Republic also has its own Supreme Soviet, separately elected, and Council of Ministers. Each province, town and county has its own soviet, which appoints an executive committee to administer the area.

The power of a Supreme Soviet or local soviet, and that of its government or executive committee, is small compared with that of the Communist Party Committee and its bureau for the same area, which operate as the superior authority and have their own staff for this purpose.

Below the county level there are the rural soviets with their executive committees, but the Communist Party does not bother much with this level of administration as it is of little importance. Matters concerning the villages are decided by the county party bureau.

GLOSSARY

USSR Union of Soviet Socialist Republics, the official name of the Russian Empire after it was reorganised into a union of republics by its Communist government in the period 1917–24. Sometimes called the Soviet Union or Soviet Russia.

Russia Often used by foreigners to mean the whole USSR. Its technical meaning is the Russian Soviet Federative Socialist Republic, the largest of the republics which constitute the USSR.

Russians Likewise often used by foreigners to mean all citizens of the USSR, almost half of whom belong to other nations.

Soviet Used adjectivally for the USSR (e.g. the Soviet government, the Soviet economy). As a noun its precise meaning is 'council'. Local soviets of workers and soldiers appeared spontaneously early in 1917 and the Bolsheviks seized power in their name.

Bolshevik As a noun—a member of Lenin's section of the Russian revolutionary movement, which took power in November 1917; as an adjective—used historically of the government formed by Lenin.

Government Sometimes used in this book to denote the central political authority, which in practice consists of the Communist Party leaders.

Marxism May mean either the doctrines of Karl Marx (1818–83), or of him and his collaborator Engels (1820–95), or the elements common to the official theories of all present-day communist countries, or present-day official theory in the USSR, or the ideas of Marx and Engels as interpreted by anybody.

Soviet Marxism This term is not used in the USSR, as it implies that there can be other kinds of genuine Marxism.

Marxism-Leninism This term is used in the USSR to denote Soviet official theory, sometimes in its general principles and sometimes in its details at any particular time.

Communism (a) Marx referred to the lower stage of communism, now called socialism, and the higher stage, now called Communism or Full Communism.

(b) The political movement to establish a Communist world (hence, Communist Party).

Socialism The nature of society after capitalism and before Full Communism. The economy is publicly owned, but people are paid according to their work. Everybody must work well, study and acquire the new moral principles so as to speed the transition to Full Communism.

Full Communism When society is rich enough for everybody to receive according to needs, and civilised enough for everybody to work well without having to earn anything. This type of society will in the main be achieved by 1980 in the USSR, according to the programme which the Communist Party adopted in 1961.

CPSU Communist Party of the Soviet Union.

KGB Committee of State Safety. Its staff is often referred to as the secret police or political police, as distinct from the ordinary police (militia).

Public Mental Life

The government of the USSR expects all citizens to know and to believe in a set of ideas called Marxism-Leninism, and does everything possible to make sure that they do so. Since the government is a powerful and determined one, and has many means of influencing people's minds, the consequences on the everyday life of the citizens are considerable. The system of ideas is more comprehensive and elaborate than any of the world's traditional religions or philosophical systems. It is not easy for the nearly 240 million inhabitants, with very different levels of education and belonging to many nations of very different backgrounds, traditions and religions to fulfil this expectation. Nevertheless, the Soviet government acts on the assumption that this aim is perfectly reasonable and that it is, indeed, already largely achieved, except for the survival of religious ideas inside the country and the influence of foreign ideas.

The Russians as a nation have a strong tradition of thinking alike. In Tsarist times it was abnormal to be a Russian without being of the Russian Orthodox religion. Ordinary people could not understand how a person could be the one without the other. So, although Tsarist governments regarded it as one of their primary duties to ensure that the faith and nationality were coextensive, they did not normally need to do much about it. The Communist government has taken over this view of right-thinking, but in respect of its own set of ideas. There are, however, important differences. The Communist ideas include philosophy, history, economics and politics, but do not provide for the personal needs of prayer and consolation. Orthodox Christianity is as old as the Russian nation itself, while Marxism was known only to a few thousand people in Russia at the time of the revolution 50 years ago. Further, attempts in Tsarist times to extend the Russian religion to other distinct nations of the Empire were restricted, in the main, to Christian nations and were not always

Map to illustrate the Note on Administrative Areas and Levels. A
Autonomous Republic is shown as an example of the twenty suc
included (*Tula* near *Moscow* and *Krasnoyarsk* in Siberia). *Towr*

P U B L I C

B E R I A

K R A S N O Y A R S K

LAKE
BAIKAL

CHINA

MONGOLIA

KOREA

JAPAN

Borders of USSR
Borders of Union Republics
Province Borders
Permafrost line
Mountain ranges

0 mls approx.   500   1000

teen Republics are shown. Within the Russian Republic the Tatar
publics in the U S S R, and two of the many provinces are also
entioned in this book are also shown

vigorously pursued. Nowadays, however, all must be or become Communist—the Moslem Turkic and Tajik peoples, the Buddhist Mongolians and the Jews, as well as the Catholic Lithuanians and Lutheran Estonians. Moreover, in 1961 the Soviet government made it a matter of great urgency to have all its citizens adhering to the official ideas because in that year it committed itself to the coming of Full Communism, which involves universal active belief in Communist ideas, by 1980.

The effect of all this on the life of the country is fourfold. Firstly, the newspapers, radio, television, films, theatre, literature, trade union meetings, entertainments and all other media of public communication are used for a didactic purpose. Thus, all domestic and foreign news is slanted in accordance with the system of ideas. Secondly, the educational services, from nursery schools to postgraduate studies, are used to inculcate the mental system, both by presenting subjects of study in accordance with it and by making Marxism-Leninism one of the subjects taught. Thirdly, a special network of adult educational institutions exists, from workers' circles to the Higher Party Schools, for instruction in Marxism-Leninism which at its lower levels involves about a quarter of the working population at any one time. Fourthly, daily life is affected by the many ways in which the authorities seek to prevent any expression of ideas which conflict with the official ones, or any criticism of them.

Fifty years is long enough to have made the Soviet population accustomed to the existence of an official view, which they are supposed to know and share, on almost everything from such large matters as the nature of the universe and the history and future of man to the latest events at home and abroad. Inhabitants of the

May Day in Moscow. One of the posters reads: 'Peoples of all countries! Fight for Peace, for universal and total disarmament. Resolutely expose the Imperialist pyromaniacs of war, the most evil enemies of Mankind!'

'Lenin lives always'

USSR—whether the man in the street, the political leaders in Moscow, or local officials responsible for the control of ideas—are not less human than anybody else. Soviet politicians and officials have their problems in this field, as in every other, and try to cope, well or badly, as do all politicians and officials in any country. Some members of the public chafe at mental guidance and restrictions, some are bitter about it, some do what they can against it, many find life easier for not having to make up their own minds, many remain indifferent and try to let the whole thing pass over their heads, while some have or need to have the deep satisfaction of a positive meaning in life through these ideas.

As an example of the last attitude, here is a letter sent by a Russian woman teacher of Marxist philosophy to a Scottish girl of 14, to whom she had sent a present of the famous autobiographical novel *How the Steel was Tempered*, written by a young Russian Communist about his life during the civil war and the early years of reconstruction. The Scottish girl had criticised the hero's passionate assumption of his duty to interfere in other people's lives for the good of the cause. The letter was written in 1961.

Dear Jenny,

My fine bluebell, you haven't been upset at my not being able to write for so long? But today I'm going to write you more than just a letter.

So, quite a lot of your last letter was about your thoughts on the character Pavel Korchagin, on the Communists and the role of the Communist Party. I read it all very attentively and although I didn't agree with it all, at first I didn't want to dispute with you as I was afraid you might misunderstand me and might even feel insulted. But the more I thought about it, the more clearly I understood that either I write to you truthfully on everything or not at all.

You and I evaluate the depiction of Pavel differently. I love him deeply. He is the beloved hero of my youth. I love him because he is simple and modest, serving the people without posing or fine words, putting everything he has into this service. I love him for his good sense, honesty, for not making concessions to enemies.

You don't like Pavel for devoting everything in his life to the people and the party. I don't understand in what service one can live more beautifully in the world. Cats and dogs live—they eat, drink, sleep, breed. They live for themselves. They don't care about anybody but themselves and their offspring. There are people who live something like that. But can one call it a really human life? Human life is work, activity, inspiration by beautiful and noble aims and aspirations.

And what can be more noble than the aspiration to serve the people? But it is not enough to want to do this, one must know how to serve. We have an amusing folk story about Ivan, who wanted to be useful to people, but didn't know how. He did and said things that were just not right, so he got badly in everybody's way and was beaten up. To avoid doing that, it is essential to understand what people need, where one can really be useful to them, and for this one must know the laws of development of society and act in accordance with them.

The laws of development of society are disclosed by historical materialism—a science created by Marx-Engels-Lenin. Historical materialism shows the conformity to law and the inevitability of the replacement of capitalism by Communism—a society in which the means of production are owned collectively, by the whole people, in which there will be no exploitation of people, in which all the conditions will be established for all-round development of personality, in which people will receive from society everything they need, to the extent needed.

But this society doesn't arise by an order from God. It has to be fought for. The paths and methods of the struggle for Communism are told in the theory of Scientific Communism, which follows from historical materialism. People deeply convinced of the correctness of this theory joined together, in order to

On the way to see Lenin's tomb

make the doctrine of Marxism known to the working people, in order to show them the way to socialism and to transform socialism and Communism from dreams of Utopian writers into reality. They called their organisation the Communist Party.

The party is a voluntary organisation of people, a united society of ideas. Nobody is compelled to join the party and the party gives its members no material privileges—no high posts, no big wages, but demands much from party members. And all the same, the ranks of the party grow, now there are over nine million members in our country. Why is this? I will show you from the example of myself: I joined the party, firstly because I believe in the victory of what it stands for, secondly because it filled my own life with great things and gave me good, genuine comrades.

Understand me, Jenny, the party is for me the most precious thing in life, it has fused for me with the idea of motherland, people, conscience and honour. Of course, in our party, as in any big organisation, there are dishonest and dishonourable people, but these are accidental to the party and they don't stay in it long. The real party member is a tough and devoted fighter for Communism. Party members are not holy or fanatics, but neither are they 'couldn't-careless' types. People who don't care have no place in the party, because it is too active and militant an organisation for them.

It seems strange and even disturbing to you that Pavel does only what the party instructs him to do. The 'instructions' of the party are special instructions. The party doesn't order, but convinces people in the rightness of what it stands for, and when a person is convinced, then what the party stands for is what he stands for. The instructions of the party fuse with his own convictions, they become his *free* choice, which makes him ready for great feats, heroism or death.

You, Jenny, think that the party has already served its purpose in our country. This is far from the case. The task of Communists is not completed by making a revolution, just as the task of builders is not completed by destroying the old building. We Communists are creators, our chief task is to build the new society. So the revolution is not the end but the beginning of a great and complicated road. This road is mapped well and clearly in the new programme of the party.

Well, to end up, about people like Pavel. You think they belong only in the revolution, but in peaceful life with its comforts they don't fit? Why do you think so? What is this 'comfort', in which people of ability, honour and principle have no place? Maybe you mean not comfort but 'couldn't care less'—that sticky swamp which drags people into the world of self, limits all their dreams to the getting of personal satisfaction? Yes, in such 'comfort' Pavel could not have lived, he was its enemy. But Pavel, like all Communists, saw the revolution as only a means for radical betterment of life in the whole country. We are in favour of comfort, we are moving towards a standard of living for everybody which the ordinary person cannot dream of under capitalism (we already have no taxes, the working day is six or seven hours, education is free, students get grants, etc.), but not for lazy enjoyment, sleeping by the stove.

The development of humanity is a struggle to transform society, to master nature completely, to take charge of the universe. And on this road the Pavels will always be needed, for their courage, energy, decisiveness, their absence of fear of difficulties, for the fire of their faith in man. The Pavels live and are active today: they plough the virgin lands, master the Arctic, work in the Brigades of Communist Labour and in the youth militia auxiliaries. We recognise the features of Pavel in Oleg Koshevoi and Zoya Kosmodemyanskaya [young hero and heroine of the Soviet-German war], in Yuri Gagarin [first man in space], in Gitalov [famous tractor driver]. There will be Pavels in the future, so long as young people are moved by great aims. The story of Korchagin is the story of how an ordinary lad becomes, under the influence of Communist ideas, a hero, a steel soldier of our party.

Well, it looks as if my letter has become a political treatise, but that, Jenny is really due to you. I haven't space left even to ask you how you spent the summer (you haven't injured yourself again?), and how you're studying now. When you have time do write to me, but don't scold me if my letter seems sharp to you — it's hard to write without passion about the most important thing in life.

With a kiss for my clever girl,
Lydia Komarova

An old woman waiting to see Lenin's tomb

There is some element of this attitude in the minds of a great many people. Even those who are most against the official ideas tend to take some aspects of them for granted, partly because Marxism-Leninism is, unlike the traditional religions, a product of the modern world, partly because it has become closely interwoven with Russian or Soviet patriotism, and partly because access to other ideas is still difficult and dangerous.

Writing in 1960, a young Russian mathematician and poet, Alexander Yesenin-Volpin, said that every Soviet person who managed to work out his own views was a Columbus. This is no longer true to the same extent, as there is now more access to foreign books and to the writings of pre-revolutionary Russian thinkers, and perhaps less fear of discussing fundamental matters with friends. Yesenin-Volpin also declared, in the same essay on his personal philosophy (which was published abroad, under his own name), that however controlled the Soviet press may be, thought is free. This was true in his case, because he insisted on thinking for himself, despite prison sentences and detention in an asylum for such words as 'an alien power . . . an alien faith, an alien law' in one of his poems. Now, a few years later, thought is free a little more easily. Those who want to can more easily retain the independence of their own minds because more people want to do so. There is a trend amongst educated people towards more critical thinking on all the basic questions to which Marxism-Leninism offers a ready-made answer. This tendency is mainly due to the need for initiative and independent judgement in modern conditions, while at the same time the authorities in charge of ideas and propaganda are finding it more difficult to present everything that happens, including the movement of thought amongst scientists, in conformity with the official scheme.

Unavoidably, this trend is meeting great obstacles and setbacks. So heavy is the censorship that anything which appears in print has some kind of official status—which makes the censors all the more thorough and their function all the more necessary from the official point of view. The Communist Party's only authority for its right to monopolise power is its claim to interpret Marxism-Leninism correctly in guiding the country to Full Communism, so any discussion or statement which looks remotely like questioning the validity of Marxism-Leninism or the moral nobility of Communism must be prevented or punished as a kind of traitorous action. There are many other reasons why the groundswell of mental freedom generates a counter-current of repression. All this is well understood in the USSR, but educated opinion there was nevertheless sickened by the government's decision to make an example of two Moscow literary men, Sinyavsky and Daniel, for writing some short stories which were published abroad. These writings were unrestrained experiments in fantastic styles to match the fantastic situations that occur in the USSR. The public prosecutor frequently used the word 'blasphemous' at the trial in February 1966. The two men were sentenced to seven and five years' imprisonment respectively. To do this must have been a difficult decision for the government. But the political police, whose influence on policy is increasing in the present circumstances, are well aware that it was writers who set the match to the Hungarian torch in 1956 and that such writings as these stories, which were getting back into the USSR, can break a brittle loyalty to the official ideas. Other people have since been sentenced, for circulating a transcript of the Sinyavsky-Daniel trial and for criticising local leaders. The practice of locking up dissidents in mental asylums has increased, and Yesenin-Volpin was again dealt with in this way early in 1968. This time, however, many distinguished Soviet scientists have signed protests on his behalf. They are the kind of people whose work the government cannot do without. There is now a continuous chain of protest on such matters, directly linking eminent scientists and scholars with the formerly quite isolated underground small groups of young intellectuals who, for this reason, cannot now be so easily disposed of by the political police.

The official set of ideas is published in many millions of copies at various levels of detail, from books in large print for people who can scarcely read to the five basic volumes for students in higher education, and in more specialist forms. The following is an outline summary of a middle-level presentation, the standard one-volume textbook for all pupils of the higher forms of secondary schools and of the junior technical colleges. This course is called 'social studies' because it includes a good deal of what we would call 'civics', such as conditions of employment in state industry and the political structure of the country, which is not strictly speaking part of Marxism-Leninism, but is presented in such a way as to fit it completely.

Summary of the School Textbook 'Social Studies' (1964 edition)

INTRODUCTION (six pages)

The present epoch of the world is that of transition to socialism and then to Full Communism, which begins the free and happy stage of human development. In our country Full Communism will be built in the main by 1980. You will spend most of your life in it and will help to develop it. This is your responsibility to history and to all future generations. You must know the science of society, or Marxism-Leninism.

Part 1   The Principles of Marxism-Leninism

Chapter 1   *Philosophy; the World and How it is Known* (35 pages)

Matter is infinite and exists independently of mind. It is always in motion—in space (change of position), and in time (development). All matter is interconnected according to ascertainable laws (i.e. the universe is a system). The most general of these laws are the three laws of dialectics: 1. Attraction and repulsion as the source of all motion, or *the unity and struggle of opposites: 2.* Gradual accumulation of change and its sudden emergence, or *transition from quantitative to qualitative change: 3.* Change, which negates a preceding condition, never negates it completely, or *negation of negation.*

Mind is a property of highly organised matter, the human brain, which 'reflects' reality. True knowledge is gained in *active* participation: in the natural sciences by experiment and in the social sciences by changing society. The results of participation (practice) are generalised by abstract thinking (theory), which is tested in more practice. Hence the unity of theory and practice.

The relation of matter to mind is the basic question of philosophy. Idealist philosophy, which is associated with religion, says mind or soul is primary. Materialist philosophy says matter is everything and mind, being a property of matter, can know everything. There is nothing outside matter, such as God, that cannot be known.

Chapter 2   *The Development of Society* (37 pages)

The determining factor in history is not ideas but the *mode of production;* this has two aspects:

(a) the technical and human *forces of production* (means of production such as tools or factories, and human skills) and (b) the legal and economic *relations of production* (e.g. between the owners of factories and the workers in factories). History (social change) is governed by the relation between (a) and (b): (a) improves with experience throughout the existence of mankind, but (b) involves social adjustment and is resistant to change. When (a) and (b) fit each other, there is relative social stability, but as change in (a) accumulates, (b) becomes increasingly out of date and must sooner or later be changed fundamentally, to give scope to the higher productivity of which (a) has become capable.

Such fundamental social change has happened four times: the change from the primitive Communism of early man (communal ownership based on the equality of poverty) to the slave system when iron tools, etc., appeared; then to serfdom; then to capitalism; and in some countries to socialism.

The part played by ideas in history is that each type of society has, in addition to its mode of production, a *superstructure* of ideas, political institutions, artistic style, religion, etc., appropriate to the preservation of the relations of production. That is, the superstructure serves the dominant (owning) class by justifying and enforcing that social system.

Great thinkers and statesmen make history by understanding its laws and operating accordingly in the superstructure to bring about necessary change. The masses make history all the time by their labour within the productive forces, which are always developing. Great artists reflect and clarify the needs and aspirations of the masses.

The basic social groups are characterised by their relation to the means of production and are called classes. The state in class society is the agency of the dominant class. In societies with antagonistic classes (slavery, serfdom and capitalism), class struggle between the exploiting and exploited classes is the engine of history. In capitalism, Marxist philosophy is the intellectual weapon of the property-less

Monopoly Capitalism – from the Social Studies *textbook*

industrial working class (the proletariat) in its class struggle. Revolution by the exploited class destroys the old social system and makes the next one possible.

Chapter 3 *Capitalism and its Decline* (26 pages)
This chapter tries to cover all the main theoretical points of Marx's *Capital* and Lenin's *Imperialism: the Highest Stage of Capitalism*. It does not do this successfully and is therefore too difficult to summarise effectively.

Chapter 4 *From Capitalism to Socialism* (12 pages)
Why the proletariat is revolutionary in all capitalist countries and the peasantry is its ally. The stages passed in Russia from the revolution in 1917 to the construction of socialism by 1936, and the great subsequent growth of productivity and production which socialism has made possible.

Part II **Socialism**
Chapter 5 *The Economic Structure of Socialism* (44 pages)
The relations of production: state and cooperative ownership of the means of production; private property in consumer goods only. Hence no exploitation. Welfare, not profit, is the aim. The law of value, commodities and money in socialism. Planning. Efficiency. Economic growth. Labour in the USSR (entering a job, conditions of employment, worker-management relations, settlement of disputes, labour discipline, the wages system).

Chapter 6 *The Social-Political Structure of Socialism* (30 pages)
'Socialism has established a new force of development, endowed with marvellous possibilities—*the social-political and mental unity of the*

entire people.' Socialist society consists of two classes—workers and peasants. Everybody else is in the stratum of white-collar occupations. There is no third class of owners and exploiters, so there are no class antagonisms. Central and local government elections, the courts rights and duties of all citizens, voluntary bodies.

Part III The Communist Party

Chapter 7 *The Party—our Steersman* (22 pages)

The party is 'the mind, honour and conscience of the present epoch'. Recent party congresses and current leaders. Its members are the most experienced and steeled citizens. The party's programme and organisation. Its policy and leadership in the construction of Full Communism.

Part IV From Socialism to Communism (116 pages)

Chapters 8–10

The economic plan for 1980. The features of Full Communism—economic, social and moral. The new Soviet man. Science, technology and productivity completely freed at last to attain their full scope in the great continuing contradiction—the unity of opposites of man and nature.

Part V Twentieth Century—
The Century of the Triumph of Communism (44 pages)

Chapters 11–12

Fraternal economic collaboration of the socialist countries. Socialist output is rapidly overtaking the output of the capitalist world. The

Planned increase in meat production – from the Social Studies *textbook. (The figures, in million tons, are quite unrealistic)*

present stage in the struggle against capitalism by the colonial peoples and by the proletariat. The great and growing strength of the USSR in the struggle for peace.

Conclusion (14 pages)

How World Communism will bring universal PEACE, satisfaction in WORK, EQUALITY, FREEDOM, BROTHERHOOD and HAPPINESS in the deepest senses in which great thinkers have form-

Annual percentage growth of industry, from the Social Studies *textbook. (The difference between Soviet and American growth-rates in the 1960s has not, in fact, been large and Japanese growth rates are a good deal higher than Soviet. The black figures are France, England and the USA, and the white one is the USSR*

ulated these age-old aspirations of mankind. (For example, in the section on Peace: contact with intelligent beings from other worlds will be friendly, because as knowledge, mastery of nature, increases, so do cooperation and goodness.)

This course in the top forms of secondary schools took up about 100 hours of teaching time when it was suddenly made compulsory in the middle of the 1962–3 school year. Since then, secondary education has been reduced by one year and this course now occupies about 70 teaching hours. The government's intention is that all children will, in a few years' time, take full secondary education, including this course. There is, however, some discussion in the educational journals on the problems of teaching the course, parts of which (philosophy and political economy in particular) are difficult even for the teachers to understand. The subject is largely taught by making pupils learn selected passages from the standard textbook. It is difficult for even the most intelligent teachers to make the theoretical parts of the course more comprehensible and the 'civics' parts more realistic, as such attempts easily lead to heretical views. For example, information on the standard of living in the United States is becoming fairly widely known and this drastically contradicts sections of Chapter 3, where the American proletariat is depicted as living in great and increasing poverty because the monopoly capitalist relations of production there hinder the forces of production. The textbook was in 1968 being very critically discussed by senior school

'No!' Anti-war poster, reproduced in the Social Studies textbook

pupils amongst themselves 'all over the country', according to an 18-year-old Russian. (This young person displayed an astonishing depth and seriousness of thought on some of the universal problems of modern life and ideas, on the basis of a narrow experience. The attempt to inculcate a modern religion may compel intelligent young people to think hard.) The pressure on school time for normal subjects makes many teachers hostile to this subject. However, they are expected to teach their own subjects as illustrations, so far as is possible, of the ideas of Marxism-Leninism. Physics and chemistry, for example, must illustrate the basic laws of dialectics. History must show the past as class struggle, with Russia and its junior partners leading the world to Communist salvation. The primary schools have no Marxism-Leninism as such, but all subjects are oriented in that direction. A book for teachers of elementary mathematics recommends them to explain to pupils how arithmetic and geometry are, in their origins, outstanding instances of the unity of theory and practice. The introduction to the 1964 edition of the standard textbook on *Geography of the USSR* for children aged 13–14 is as follows:

> Look at the map of the world: you will see that our Motherland, the Union of Soviet Socialist Republics, is the largest state on earth. . . . The natural wealth of our Motherland is varied and great. . . . It fully provides our economy with everything necessary. In our country, under the leadership of the Communist Party, a socialist society has been constructed. The USSR is the first country of

socialism in the world. . . . The Soviet people have unlimited love for their socialist Fatherland. The words of the song resound inspiringly:

> *Boundless country of my birth,*
> *Many its forests, fields and streams:*
> *No other such country do I know*
> *Where so freely man can breathe.*

We stand against war, for the preservation of enduring peace throughout the world. All the peoples of our country have one aim —to construct a Communist society, to enhance the glory and happiness of the Soviet people, to strengthen the power of the socialist state. The programme of the Communist Party of the Soviet Union solemnly declares that the present generation of Soviet people will live under Communism. In order to become builders of Communist society and bring benefit to the Motherland, it is necessary to master many branches of knowledge. The *Geography of the USSR* will give you knowledge of the natural features of our country, of its uncounted resources, and also of the brotherly friendship between the Soviet peoples and of their active economic and cultural advancement. . . .

Lower down, in the most junior classes and in the kindergartens, the same ideas and attitudes are inculcated through the appropriate media such as toys, songs, games, stories about Lenin as the perfect man, and in particular through the children's organisations (Octobrists and Young Pioneers) which are in effect part of the school system.

A large proportion of boys and girls who leave school at 15 get a more elementary course along the social studies lines in the apprenticeship institutions. The several million people of 17–18 in the junior technical colleges also take the course.

In higher education, Marxism-Leninism (under that name) is compulsory for all students. Students of the social sciences, literature, history, law and languages have four or five hours a week of lectures and seminars on it, while science and technology students have about three hours. The sequence of the subjects is: history of the CPSU; dialectical materialism (corresponding to Chapter 1 in the school textbook summarised on pp. 11–15 above); historical materialism (Chapters 2 and 4); political economy (Chapters 3 and 5); and scientific communism (Chapters 6, 8–12). Each of these five subjects has a standard textbook of up to 1,000 pages. In some institutions three shorter courses, of up to 40 teaching hours, are also given, on scientific atheism, Marxist ethics and Marxist aesthetics, which develop certain aspects of the main courses. The 'battle of the hours' over Marxism-Leninism, which is noticeable but not prominent in the secondary schools, is a marked feature of staff life in the universities and the hundreds of technological institutions of higher education. The lecturers and professors in the various sections of Marxism-Leninism, who number about 14,000, tend to be regarded by the rest of the staff as distinctly inferior in academic quality, an attitude which the great majority of them well deserve, as they are in effect official propagandists, though with the same salaries and formal status as their colleagues. The heads of these institutions often succeed in 'stealing' perhaps an hour a week from Marxism-Leninism to the benefit of the 'real' subjects, the professors of which hang on grimly to this illegal gain while the Rector spins out correspondence with the Ministry of Higher Education in the republic capital as long as possible or does his best to persuade inspectors, arriving in response to complaints from the Marxism-Leninism staff, to turn a blind eye and let him produce competent engineers or doctors.

The attitude of the students is not very different. They show distinctly less respect for the ideological staff. It is common for only the first rows at these lectures to pay attention, while those behind in the enormous lecture-halls get on with their 'real' studies. In the case of some lecturers, even the first rows do the same. Since attendance at lectures is compulsory, and lecturers can scarcely add anything not in the standard textbooks and the ancillary collections of readings from Marx, Engels, Lenin and party resolutions, only the more forceful, or those genuinely trying to get the spirit of the ideas across to the students, seriously expect their lectures to be listened to. At seminars, which usually last two hours and sometimes four, short papers on assigned topics are read out by some students and the others discuss them. These are often even more monotonous than the lectures, because the occasion invites discussion while the limits of discussion are very narrow and more or less known beforehand. Some lecturers tell students at seminars to speak their minds more freely, as the correct view (essential for passing the examination) will be made perfectly clear at the end of the seminar.

When Stalin's infallibility was officially rejected in 1956 there was panic amongst the Marxism-Leninism lecturers, as the standard texts were constructed around his statements, and the *History of the CPSU*, then the basic section of the course, placed him in the supreme historical role. Teaching in the subject virtually ceased,

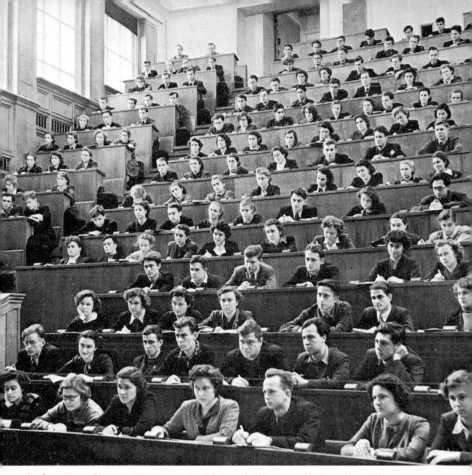

*A chemistry lecture in a new building of Moscow University. The
Deputy Rector can listen-in to any lecture in his own office*

until the Department of Social Sciences in the central Ministry of
Higher Education issued temporary notes for lectures. By the later
1950s the new standard textbooks were prepared and all was well
again. The examinations in these subjects (which are conducted
orally as in many others) sometimes jolt even an informed Western
academic visitor, on seeing the occasional intelligent student, who
refuses to give the precisely 'correct' answer, which he knows to be
illogical or false, and offers a slightly different but well-reasoned
alternative, given a mark which means failure and even loss of his
grant, while a student who is a member of the Young Communist
League Committee, and knows almost nothing, is passed with a
good margin. One examiner, who gave the highest marks to a girl

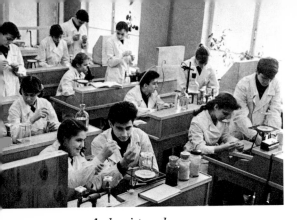

A chemistry class

who answered every question in a kind of trance, head back and eyes closed, by repeating the textbook word for word, remarked with satisfaction to the author that this was an ideal student. The normal attitude of competent students is to learn the materials and their correct current interpretation, to pass the examinations adequately and then to forget the subject more or less completely.

The insistence of the government on continuing to use a substantial proportion of students' time, and of the heavy costs of higher education, on Marxism-Leninism, is partly explained by the fact that nowadays all entry into responsible posts, including the administration of the party itself, is through higher education. Just as all schoolchildren must become good Communists, all students must become informed Communists, whether they join the party or not. This attitude goes well beyond the view that even if they do not in their hearts accept the ideas something will stick. There is a very strong tendency in the public mental life of the USSR to confuse outward with inward agreement. The *expression* of unanimity on basic philosophical matters has assumed great importance for the authorities. There is heavy pressure from leading people in the sciences and technology to drop the teaching of Marxism-Leninism, or to make it optional, in higher education. The result would be an important improvement in specialist training, or reduction in its cost, and the government must be well aware of this. Such pressure is strongest in the armed forces, where all the recruits have had to devote over 60 hours of their training time to Marxism-Leninism. Now that the great majority get a good deal of it at school, in one form or another, this may be reduced or even dropped, though it is impossible to expect 'political chats'—a more general form of the same thing, on events of the day—to be dropped in the forces. But to drop the theory which legitimates the existence of the party itself and the whole policy of the country, at the higher educational level, would mean a far more serious change—in effect that the USSR had become less concerned with its anchor in the whole past and future of man, in the depths of nature and the minds of the great thinkers of every age. It does not matter so much whether the anchor is there or is conventionally supposed to be there, but to weaken the convention would somehow be a dangerous threat to stability.

The same inability to moderate the claims of Marxism-Leninism can be seen in the press. Shortly after Stalin's death Khrushchev earnestly appealed in a public speech to the Soviet newspapers to become less monotonous. A few years later he was in supreme power, and his son-in-law became editor of the second most important newspaper, but this view was implemented only in very minor detail. The newspapers could not become lively, interesting or informative because of their function in the single mental system. They published his own frequent and long speeches in full, because as the party leader he was the public formulator of policy and interpreter of events in the light of the theory. He was, indeed, particularly prone to relate domestic policy and foreign events to the six stages of history, especially the last two—the coming transition of capitalist countries to socialism and of the USSR to Communism. Since his departure, voices have been raised at lower levels, including by writers, for a more lively press. But the old dictum, that the press is the sharpest weapon of the party, retains its supposed force, though the party's perpetual message has become blunted in the eyes of a more sophisticated public.

The newspaper *Pravda* has an editorial in its issue of 27 August 1967, of which the following sentences are typical:

. . . The greatest manliness and labour enthusiasm of millions were needed for the revolutionary transformations which completed the full and final victory of Socialism in the USSR. . . . Only free people, working for themselves, for the welfare of society and knowing the purpose of their exertions, are capable of such feats as distinguish the half-century history of the first country of socialism in the world. . . . The new generation of Soviet people guard as sacred the revolutionary and labour traditions of the fathers. . . . The energy and mind of Soviet people are directed towards achievement of the new tasks of constructing Communism set forth by the XXIII Congress of the CPSU. . . . Communism is created by the heroic labour of the people, inspired by the Communist Party. . . .

The other main item on page 1 is a statement by the Minister of the Coal Industry, headed 'To the Festival, Warriors of the Coal Front!' in connection with the annual Miners' Day, accompanied by a photograph of a record-breaking mining team. Harvesting and other economic items in similar style complete the home news on this page, for instance, 'The labouring people of agriculture in Sumi province, having developed socialist emulation so as worthily to meet the 50th anniversary of the Great October Socialist Revolution, on 25 August fulfilled the plan for sale of grain to the state by 123 per cent.' Although these items are connected with a special occasion, their style is little more high-pitched than is normal, year in and year out, and the content is the common core of public mental life on domestic matters.

Foreign news is often no less extravagant in tone. The aftermath of the Arab-Israeli war was prominently featured in the Soviet press during the same period, in line with the role of imperialism in the theory. World monopoly capitalism, intent on arresting the self-liberation of the Arabs from its imperialist exploitation, uses for this purpose the little imperialism of Israel to attack the Arabs on racial and religious pretexts. The Arab countries are weakened by division between those with revolutionary and those with reactionary (still feudal) states, and within the former there is division between the emergent capitalist class and the radical masses. The Egyptian armed forces were badly officered, by scions of the new capitalist and old feudal families: the Egyptian masses must take over from them. (At no point in this press campaign have the Jews as such been attacked. Israel is depicted as behaving like the Nazis in occupied territory, and Zionism as a sinister, secret, world-wide conspiracy with immense influence inside the United States and seeking a foothold in the USSR, but both Israel and Zionism are presented within the picture of monopoly capitalism and its imperialist necessities.) The same view of the Arab-Israeli situation was put at public meetings organised by the party throughout the country and duly reported by press and radio. The Soviet government is very reluctant to admit that public opinion is not unanimously behind its policies, in foreign affairs especially. For this reason, there has been no mention in the press of sympathy for Israel amongst Soviet Jews and others.

Soviet press treatment of Czechoslovakia in the weeks before the invasion on 21 August 1968 was even more schematic. The fact that the Czechoslovak Communist Party permitted public expression of opinion other than its own was equated with the undermining of socialism and the handing over of Czechoslovakia to the imperialist world. Not one of about 20 casual Soviet acquaintances in the USSR, with whom the author discussed Czechoslovakia at that time,

Pravda, 5 March 1968, top half of page 1. The two medals always appear because the newspaper has twice been awarded the Order of Lenin. The leader columns are occupied by a message to the party which begins: 'The XIV congress of the trade unions of the USSR in the name of 86 million trade union members and all the toilers of our country sends a fiery heartfelt greeting to our own Communist Party and its fighting general staff – the Leninist Central Committee.' The picture is of a manganese mine which has produced 40,000 tons above plan. Under the picture: *preparations for spring sowing in the Ukraine.* Top right: *three items on progress of the five-year plan: 'Gas pipeline goes through mountains', 'Bonus for economical work', 'Rainbow of Bryansk textiles'*

accepted this official view. Most of them did not have enough trustworthy information to form an opinion and were anxious to get information from foreigners.

Soviet people sometimes express surprise that foreigners read their newspapers, since the basic function of the press is to present everything in accordance with official policy and the official theory. Many Soviet newspaper readers, probably a large proportion of them, read between the lines: they use what is printed on world affairs as clues rather than information. The same is true of domestic affairs. It is only by living in the USSR for a year or two that one realises the extent to which the population is still sealed off from news. To the Westerner, who takes the supply of information for granted, it is like living in a room with no doors or windows. The chief 'window on the world' is nowadays foreign broadcasts in Russian and other Soviet languages, mainly by American and British radio services. The only foreign newspapers available to the Soviet public are Communist publications, but a small number of specialists are allowed access for their work to the important newspapers and periodicals of the non-Communist countries. The friends, and friends' friends, of these people are unusually well informed. In April 1968 the London *Times* was allowed to be sold in Moscow. However, the author tried for two weeks to buy *The Times* in Moscow, without success. Soviet students told him that they had been trying, in vain, for months.

A day in the life of a factory worker, from the point of view of news and information, would be something like this. If he or she is single and living in an industrial hostel, as many young workers do in factory towns, the room is likely to contain a loudspeaker wired to the town network. The author once lived in a hostel in Russia and could still hear the programme clearly when the room loudspeaker was switched off because it was on in other rooms. (At that time there was a party campaign against 'the silence of the loudspeakers'.) Our mythical but typical worker will hear the morning news programme, which has come from the same source (TASS, the Soviet governmental news agency) as that for the central and provincial press. He is likely to find the same wording on anything of consequence, whether he is listening to the central or local radio or reading the paper, which is delivered by the postman if he is a subscriber, or bought at a kiosk on the way to work. It is also pasted up on boards in the street. The local items in the news are almost always of production results in relation to the local plan, which is part of the national plan and this in turn is the current year's step towards Communism.

Skilled workers tend to be more clannish and less inhibited than others on political matters amongst themselves; a workmate with a good private radio (which many people have) may tell our imaginary worker of items heard about world affairs or life in Britain on the BBC Russian broadcast, or on Radio Liberty or the Voice of America about something otherwise unreported concerning the USSR. Or he may have listened to a pirate transmitter in Soviet territory broadcasting pop music interspersed with anti-party jokes and short political talks. (Those responsible are treated drastically when caught. But the authorities have few detection vans in the provinces.) A technician at the factory may have recently returned from abroad and bits of information going round the factory from that source may be chewed over. Twenty minutes of the hour's break for lunch is likely to be spent, perhaps once a week, in a 'worker's circle', at which one of the office staff may do his party duty by reading aloud some items from the day's newspaper and relating them to aspects of Marxism-Leninism. If our worker left school at 15 and, as many do, is going through the syllabus of the secondary school at an evening class attached to the factory, he may be taking a

The hand of Imperialism in Czechoslovakia is firmly arrested. This cartoon appeared in Izvestia on 22 August 1968, the day of the invasion by Warsaw Pact troops

history or literature lesson at which the ideological aspects will be stressed more strongly than for schoolchildren, or the lesson may be social studies. Alternatively, he may be attending an evening course on the theory itself, where the tutor is on the Marxism-Leninism staff of the local technical college or is a history or ideology teacher at a local school.

If a trade union meeting takes place at the factory that day, it will be convened at short notice on an important foreign or domestic political event or it will be a more routine meeting on productivity in the factory. In the first case, the meeting will begin by several speakers, who have been given the full text of what to say by the party organiser, relating the event to the world struggle between Imperialism (mainly the United States) and Progress (the socialist and colonial countries and the proletariat of the imperialist countries), and this to the 'world-historic' role of the USSR; the meeting will conclude with promises of better production, as the contribution of those present to the struggle. If it is a routine production meeting, there will be stress on greater productivity as the reason why one social system replaces another. Any Soviet pronouncement or speech or ceremony of special importance will be heard from loudspeakers in the factory or the street. If the evening is spent at a cinema or theatre, the film or play will have been most thoroughly vetted by ideological experts to ensure that it contributes to the general official message, and by censorship officials to ensure that it does not in any way contradict the message. Nowadays more pre-revolutionary plays and foreign films are being shown, but the selection and presentation of these, too, is closely controlled.

If our worker is a party member, it will be his responsibility to provide his workmates with correct ideas. But few manual workers stand higher in the party than rank-and-file membership, and he is unlikely to be very different from his workmates in such a human matter as information. Nowadays, however, a worker who joins the party is apt to be regarded as a careerist by his mates and not to be quite trusted by them. A party membership card is called a 'bread card'. If he is an informer, which has little to do with whether he is in the party or not, his workmates are likely to know or suspect. If he has joined the party within the past year or two, he will almost certainly be attending a course for members in Marxism-Leninism and, in that connection, will be learning how to discuss current affairs with friends and workmates. The usual form of such a course is one evening a week for a year, but there are many repetition courses. During 1966–7, over eight million people were attending such courses, which is over half the total membership of the party.

There is also a special network of party schools for more thorough study of the theory and its relation to current events and to policy and long-term trends in all spheres. These are for members who are becoming senior local officials, or central officials, of either the governmental or party structure. The courses are full-time and last from two to four years; those selected to attend continue to receive their full salaries, which are usually high. The period spent on Marxism-Leninism itself in these institutions is between 800 and 1,300 class hours. About 12,000 persons, usually in their thirties or early forties, complete these courses each year. Almost all have already had a higher education, in which the compulsory Marxism-Leninism courses have provided a substantial basis for their present advanced studies. The attitude of mind in these studies is that of people in the know. They are men (few women reach this stage of political responsibility) who have already exercised authority and power in the service of Communism. The system of ideas is of the greatest importance to them, since the meaning of their functions and careers, their self-confidence and self-respect are bound up with it. They see themselves as controlling the progress of their country towards Full Communism and thereby heavily influencing, directly or indirectly, the transition of the whole world in that direction.

The date 1980 was never of particular importance to these people. They knew that so rapid an attainment of Full Communism was propagandist and unrealistic. They know a great deal about the real strengths and weaknesses of their country, the rest of the socialist world, and the realities of other countries. They also know that there may be very great difficulties and setbacks, but these do not basically matter either, in the light of all history, which is on their side, as is the nature of reality, which they know from dialectical materialism. They are servants of science, the science of society, with its immutable laws that were discovered once and for all by Marx, and this service is given through the Communist Party of the USSR. Science must take new phenomena into account, but not to the extent of weakening their own confidence in Marxism-Leninism or allowing the disagreeable questionings of writers and other irresponsible intellectuals to upset the masses, or factory managers to make too many decisions on their own.

2

The Political and Economic Framework

THE PAST ALIVE IN THE PRESENT

The present political and economic structure was built up, in the main, during the first 20 years of the Soviet regime. It was administered very harshly under Stalin's personal dictatorship. Under his successors the system has been little changed, but the severity of its administration has been modified, mainly by a reduction in the power of the political police and fairer treatment of the peasants.

During Stalin's period of supreme power, which lasted from the early 1930s until his death in 1953, the political police arrested millions of people on suspicion of disloyalty to his regime or of heresy, or even without such suspicion, simply because it was their function to do so. The worst period was the 'great purge' of 1936–8. This was not an isolated nightmare. It was the peak of a process of exiling, imprisoning or executing opponents which began immediately after the Bolshevik revolution. It was first used against political opponents of the party. When these could no longer be considered a serious danger, it was used by Stalin and his followers against their opponents within the party and, on a far greater scale, against the peasants from the winter of 1929–30 onwards. When both the politicians and the peasants were cowed, by the middle 1930s, the process appeared to get suddenly out of hand in the autumn of 1936. The author, who was living in Russia at that time, saw this happen. The number of arrests, the fear of arrest, and fear of saying or doing anything that might conceivably be misconstrued, became so great that by the summer of 1937 it was hard to see how administration and industrial production could continue. The storm began to abate in 1938. By then, the generation of Bolsheviks who had made the revolution in 1917 and consolidated it during the 1920s had been virtually eliminated. With them, a very large proportion of all the educated people had also gone. The vacant political, managerial and

28

Moscow: May Day procession

professional posts were taken over by 'pushed-up' younger men from the working class. (In the author's experience, these men, ignorant but practical, believed in Stalin as a very great leader and thinker and formed the basis of his power. They were the most energetic and competent of the working-class and peasant youngsters who had come into the party during the 1920s.)

During the war, the great number of further arrests, and such associated events as the sudden deportation of seven small nations from areas reached or nearly reached by the Germans, expressed the same attitude of suspicion and rule by terror, now directed mainly against possible lack of patriotic ardour. For the same reason, Soviet troops who had been captured in large numbers by the Germans early in the war were liable to be sent to labour camps after the war, though the fault for the early defeats was that of their government and generals. The last intensification of the terror system, in 1951–3, showed signs of repeating the scale of the great prewar purge, but was curtailed by Stalin's death, whereupon the party leaders who might themselves have perished in the last purge and who understood that the country could not continue to be ruled in this way, broke the special power of the political police.

It was widely felt in the USSR that the death of Stalin marked the end of the Soviet Union's iron age, but such a feeling had also been widespread in 1945 when the war was won. Stalin had soon dispelled that expectation when he declared that the economy must be very quickly reconstructed and expanded until the country was strong enough to withstand any further attack, a process which he said would take at least 15 years. When he died the reconstruction and expansion had in fact proceeded faster than he had indicated, but the economy was very heavily overweighted in a military direction. It was the general feeling that further growth was being hindered by the harsh personal dictatorship and concentration upon armaments that led people to anticipate a relaxation in 1953. The first important economic step taken by the coalition of party leaders which succeeded Stalin was to raise the prices paid by the state to the collective farms for agricultural products.

During 1917 the landed estates had been seized by the peasants, so as to enlarge their own small family farms. The Bolshevik government, which had no sympathy for the peasants but needed their support, legalised this and encouraged it to continue. The result, after the civil war, was about 20 million small family farms, mostly run on the old strip system (like the pre-enclosure farms in England), which would provide a surplus for feeding the towns and for exports only if the peasants thought it worth their while. This situation could not indefinitely be accepted by the Bolsheviks. In their uneasy truce with the peasantry during the 1920s they became convinced that the only way to consolidate their power and carry out their programme of modernising Russia by socialist planning was to gain direct control over everything of importance, especially the food supplies. (In the event, they did this so thoroughly that they gained direct control over the population, too.)

Stalin, when by 1929 the party and political police had become sufficiently organised and responsive to his personal direction, solved this problem by declaring the more successful and influential peasants (the so-called *kulaks*) to be enemies of the regime, who were to be 'liquidated as a class', leaving the 'middle' and 'poor' peasants to join their lands into collective farms. Any peasant who stood out against collectivisation was termed a 'kulak' or 'sub-kulak' or 'pro-kulak' and many of these shared the same fate—mass deportation to poor lands or labour camps, hundreds or thousands of miles

Crimea farmyard

away. A local police report in 1930 noted that, whereas it had formerly taken several police to arrest one peasant, a group of peasants could now be taken away by one policeman. The collectivisation broke the spirit of the peasantry as a whole, and this moral destruction was completed by the deaths of several million peasants in 1932–3, in a famine, due mainly to the collectivisation. The peasantry ceased to be a social, political or economic factor, for the government could now take what it wanted from the quarter of a million collective farms, instead of having to be careful about taxes and prices in relation to 20 million independent farms. The poverty of the new collective farms was made worse by the loss of the most efficient peasants, who had been deported, and of half the farm animals, including most of the horses, which had been slaughtered by their embittered owners before they could be collectivised.

Until Stalin's death the collective farms were at the mercy of party officials in the county towns and the heads of the government's machine-tractor stations; the main function of these men was to obtain the required produce, whether as 'compulsory deliveries', taxes or payment in kind for the services of tractors and other machinery. The state paid the farms for the compulsory deliveries, but so little for most products that agriculture in effect fell out of the monetary system, except for the selling of produce to townspeople by farms near enough to do so. It was not until the autumn of 1953 that agriculture as a whole began to be brought back into the monetary system by an increase of state payments for the compulsory deliveries.

By 1956, when the party leaders publicly announced that Stalin had made mistakes in his treatment of the peasantry and in rule by terror, the two worst features of Stalinism in the villages and towns were being rectified: the collective farms were being much better paid for many of their products and almost all the surviving political prisoners in the labour camps had been released. The worst of the terror and of the new peasant serfdom was over, but the memory of these sufferings is still very strong. This memory, mingled with some

apprehension, is a most important factor in the present-day life of all but the younger generation of Soviet people. At the time of collectivisation three-quarters of the total population were peasants. And there is scarcely a family in the town population of Stalin's time which did not have at least one member or relative arrested. These facts of recent history, taken together with the poverty, the harshness of industrial discipline, the thought-control and the almost incredible overcrowding in the towns during the Stalin period, explain why the question of 'de-Stalinisation'—a term not used

Boys requesting souvenirs from travellers at a Siberian railway station

in the USSR—still matters so much to people there 15 years after his death. The political and economic framework within which these things happened—and within which the USSR became the second power in the world—is still, in all essentials, the same.

POLITICS AT THE TOP

In political life the dominant and indeed the only permitted factor is the Communist Party. There are other political organisations, which aspire to overthrow the Communist Party, but very little is known about them. They probably consist of scattered and very small groups, possibly influenced by anti-communist émigré organisations, of which the best known is the NTS (People's Labour Union). Gerald Brooke, the Englishman who was sentenced to five years in a Soviet labour camp in 1965, was arrested when delivering literature which he had brought into the country on behalf of the NTS. It is perfectly possible that there are more members of the Soviet political police engaged in tracing NTS sympathisers in the USSR than there

are of the latter. The Communist Party justifies its right to the
monopoly of political power by the fact that it was founded by
Lenin, who is officially regarded as the only infallible disciple of
Marx, and that the party itself is infallible in applying the science of
Marxism-Leninism to the practice of government. It is recognised as
possible that a leader of the party, other than Lenin, may make
mistakes, but there is some mystical sense in which the party as such
cannot be wrong. After Khrushchev, it is held that collective leadership has been established, which makes it less likely that leaders'
decisions can be erroneous. (It was also held, after Stalin's death,
that collective leadership had been established.)

The party congress, which now meets every four years, is the
highest authority. This congress nowadays consists of about 4,000
persons, who are senior officials of the party and the state at the central
and higher local levels, with a sprinkling of other members from
science, the arts, factories, farms, transport and the forces to provide a
conventional appearance of representing the 13 million members.
These delegates are elected—but by prior arrangement as to who shall
be elected—at local and army party conferences. The proceedings at
congresses follow the pattern established under Stalin, of long
reports by the central leaders on foreign and internal policy since the
preceding congress. Discussion on these reports amounts to local
party leaders and ministers for particular industries reviewing
progress in their spheres of responsibility. Most of these contributions
from the floor are by the party leaders of provinces, large towns and
small republics, and are arranged in an almost identical way, dealing
first with the industry of the area, then the agriculture and then
various other matters. Thus, a congress consists essentially of two
parts: about half a dozen long reports on national and international
matters and up to 100 progress reports on the economy of each area.

Differences of opinion on anything more political than, say, the
location of a big new factory, are never openly expressed and even
such minor differences are rare. The leaders' reports and the resolutions are always adopted unanimously and there is heavy applause at
conventional points in the proceedings, which are held in a hall
completely dominated by a gigantic representation of Lenin. The
atmosphere is one of extreme stability, the delegates and speeches
being in an established mould, and at the same time it is dynamic
along set lines, in the central and local reports on the progress of
production—like a heavy train moving powerfully and even majesti-
cally along a track. If anything unusual is to take place, it is at a

closed session, from which the fraternal foreign delegates and the press are excluded. Khrushchev's criticism of Stalin in 1956 was made at such a session and has never been published in the USSR. A party congress is a political occasion mainly in the sense of political ceremony, a demonstration of unanimity and progress every four years by all the important people in the country. It is reported in the press, at public mass meetings, on radio and television and in the news films in this spirit. There was something about the last party congress, in 1966, however, which made it different from its predecessors. It had lost the touch of grandeur and majesty. Not only were the jokes made about it more open than on previous occasions, but they reflected this change.

Sessions of the Supreme Soviet of the USSR, whose members are elected directly by the population every four years and which is the supreme legislative body of the state, corresponding to Parliament in Britain, have a similar but less weighty ceremoniousness. The Supreme Soviet meets two or three times a year for a few days and formally approves such matters as the annual budget, economic plan, new laws and amendments to the constitution. The Soviet press is at the time of writing popularising the fact that the Supreme Soviet has many special commissions on various matters, which carefully scrutinise and alter projects for new laws or other matters submitted by the government. However, nobody suggests that such amendments are more than marginal, or that decisions of any importance are made without the authority of the party leaders. There is, theoretically, always a possibility that the Supreme Soviet may become a genuine parliament, but the entire political atmosphere of control by the party leaders would have to change first, as well as the mode of election to the Supreme Soviet. It has never been known, since the first elections under the 1936 Constitution, for more than one candidate to stand in any constituency, or for less than about 99 per cent of the electorate to vote for that candidate, or for any member of the Supreme Soviet to vote against a measure or even abstain, or for the membership of the Supreme Soviet not to conform to the plan issued from party headquarters—so many members from each occupation, a certain proportion of men to women, party members to non-members, and so on.

Some foreign observers have been surprised at the genuine sense of festivity which they have seen amongst the voters at an election to the Supreme Soviet, without realising that on such occasions the authorities increase the amount of goods available in the shops. (A

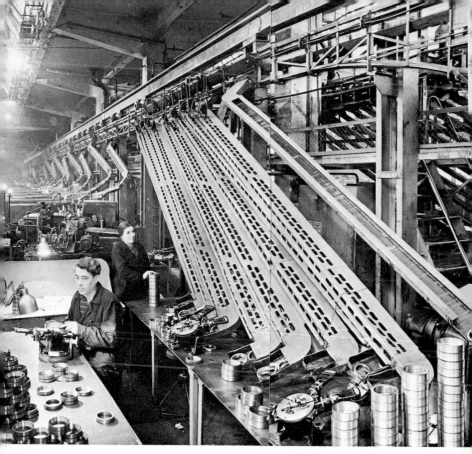

Automatic machine line at the largest bearings plant. (It proved a costly lesson in how not to introduce automation)

Soviet group touring Britain when the 1964 election campaign was in progress were told by their interpreter that the Conservative Party had arranged for the shops to be well stocked.) An election is also important for the ordinary Soviet voter, especially if he is a Russian, as a demonstration of the underlying unity of his country in face of the outer world. It is also his only means of participation in the political life of the country as a whole, even though the means are entirely conventional. An election is a challenge to the local organisations of the party, in particular to their agitation and propaganda departments, to make sure that everybody votes. Ballot-boxes are taken to those too old or ill to go to the polling station, and to the passengers on long-distance trains. It is a seriously unpatriotic act not to vote.

A friend of the author, who was a member of an electoral

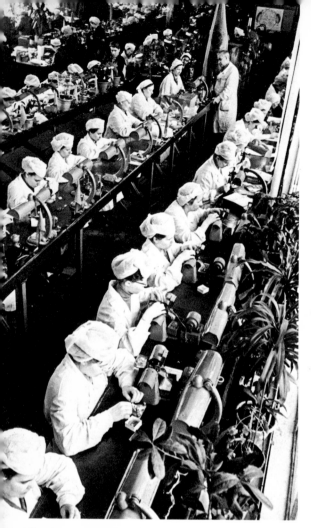

The Soviet watch factories are an example of speed and success in developing the manufacture of consumer goods if sufficient investment and good managers and technicians are provided

commission responsible for the proper conduct of an election in one of the new territories after the war, describes how the province party office demanded that the election be completed, with 100 per cent turnout, by midday instead of 10 p.m. This was done, with great exertion, by bringing in most of the people to vote and by members of the commission themselves voting on behalf of the remainder. This man himself disposed of about 500 ballot-papers. The chairman of the commission, in order to obviate hostile remarks on the ballot-papers, went round all the polling booths and broke the points of the pencils provided. (He could not remove them, as they have to be available by electoral law, although there is only one name on the ballot-paper.) This commission telephoned the party office to announce completion by midday, only to learn that a neighbouring constituency had completed its task earlier, by starting on the previous day. Such flagrant actions do not occur in more settled times, but this episode does indicate the element of unreality in elections to the Supreme Soviet. Voters who have nothing to hide do not go behind the curtain provided, where they could cross out the single name or write a hostile comment, but fold the ballot-paper in full sight and drop it in the box.

In the complete absence of public comment or analysis about the top political level, there is plenty of gossip and rumour on the attitude of party leaders to each other and to particular policies. One also meets an opinion that the actual centre of power is an undefined group of elderly people, some of them retired, whose background is quite varied. Perhaps not more than half of them are members of the highest party or state bodies. They form a kind of social apex at the top of the upper class. Their children and grandchildren tend to intermarry. To gain the good will of this society is a decisive step in a political career. Policy documents prepared by the higher staff of the party are not necessarily seen by all these people, but the action taken will be in line with the consensus of their views. The existence of this 'power club' may well be a myth. The author has not been able to get a list of names—apart from the obvious ones —from anybody who thinks it is a political fact. The 'club' has been described in terms which would almost include one or two of the actual heads of the Russian Orthodox Church as quasi-members of it. It is mentioned here to indicate the way some Soviet people think they are governed, rather than as a fact. In the government of any country there must be something in the nature of a consensus of the most influential, experienced and well-connected people which does not entirely lie within the framework of established institutions. What the writer has been told, however, is that the Soviet 'club' is something more than this—a very tight social group of elderly people whose values and outlook are not very different from those of Stalin, in whose service their careers were made. Some Russians with whom the 'club' theory has been discussed say it is nonsense.

The Central Committee of the party, which has about 200 full members, is elected at the party congress and in turn nominates the Politbureau as its small day-to-day executive. The Politbureau usually consists of about 11 members: the number is never an even one, in order to obviate the deadlock of an equal vote. Almost all members of the Central Committee are preordained, in the sense that the men who have reached certain levels of central and local party leadership become its members, together with some generals, scientists, writers and industrialists who have special organisational responsibility or symbolical importance in their spheres. Its members include nearly all the party leaders of republics, provinces and the largest towns and senior central officials such as heads of the departments of the Central Committee. It meets three or four times a year, its agendas and some of its decisions are published in the press, and sometimes a report of its proceedings is issued. These reports are the nearest

Soviet equivalent to the British *Hansard*, for the Central Committee is far more important than the Supreme Soviet. However, since the central party officials and local party leaders who constitute the main membership of the CC are themselves appointed to these posts by the Politbureau, or the dominant faction in it, Soviet citizens who are interested in politics still do not know how the question of power is handled at these high levels.

They do know that the Central Committee has a very large staff. This staff is organised in departments for cadres (personnel), ideology (formulation and dissemination of Marxism-Leninism), education, science, the party organisation itself (this department is also responsible for the Young Communist League as the youth arm of the party and the trade unions as its labour arm), culture (literature, the arts, libraries and entertainments), the armed forces, political police, security and espionage generally, agriculture, heavy industry and construction, manufactured consumer goods, foreign policy, relations with foreign Communist parties, and a few others. The senior officials of these CC departments number about 300 and probably constitute the key group of 'civil servants' in the entire system of government and decision-making. Everything of any importance passes through their hands. They prepare the agendas, information and recommendations for the Central Committee (of which many of them are members) and for the Politbureau. To get the ear of one of these people is to have one's business magically facilitated. The Politbureau, for example, decides expenditures of foreign currency, down to surprisingly small items. Most of such decisions are very brief: they depend on the materials prepared by these men. The CC departments are controlled by the Secretariat of the CC, a body about the same size as the Politbureau and not much inferior to it in importance. Under Stalin's personal domination of all the key bodies, the Secretariat may for long periods have been more important than the Politbureau.

A department of the Central Committee, because it bears the basic responsibility for everything within its sphere, must decide—subject to the Secretariat or the Politbureau in specially important cases—who occupies any post of consequence within that sphere. Thus, a party member whose career is progressing well in any field is liable to be 'called to the CC' for interview at the relevant department and told he has been selected for a certain post—say, editor of a republic newspaper or chief engineer of a big factory. To be 'called' is itself a mark of distinction for a youngish man. Sometimes, however, an older man may not want to take the suggested post. It is the author's impression, from the odd bits of information that filter through on such matters, that the economic departments of the CC are less dictatorial in these appointments than are the political departments, and that the latter were more prepared before the war to take their nominees' preferences into account than they are now. One man 'called' recently to the ideology department refused the proffered post and had a heart attack when told to hand over his party membership card; he eventually went to the post. Military appointments of any importance are always made jointly by the armed forces department of the CC and the General Staff.

Making bicycles in a corner of a motor car works

LOCAL PARTY LEADERSHIP

At every level down to the small towns and counties, the system of appointments for whatever are deemed key posts on the local scale is the same, in that it is done by the local party leaders and their staffs. At every level there is a list of posts and a list of certain party members. This is the *nomenklatura*, one of the key words in the Soviet political world. A man or woman on the local nomenklatura is one sufficiently trusted by the local party chiefs, and sufficiently experienced in what the party wants, to be sent to any post on the list, whether it is head of a school, farm, factory, cinema, county newspaper or rural soviet. Some of these appointments are supposed to be made by the administrative authorities, such as the county education office, and others by collective farmers or local citizens in an election;

the party's choice may meet with their resistance. Nowadays, with professional competence becoming increasingly important, the local party chiefs do not always get their first choice through. But they have the final effective responsibility for such appointments, because they are responsible to their own superiors in the party hierarchy for everything in their area. The nomenklatura is divided into posts for which the party selects the holder and posts which are filled by the relevant administrative authority, but with the party's agreement. Nomenklatura jobs are always well paid, relative to others in the area, and to be thrown off the list is usually a financial as well as a social and political disaster; one becomes just an ordinary party member, with little prospect of rising again.

There is one overriding criterion for getting on to the local nomenklatura, staying on it or climbing to one at a higher level: the ability to make things easy for one's party chief at the particular level. He is a man of many responsibilities, his function is to show good reports to his own party superiors about everything in his area and his aim is to secure a reputation with them for dependability and no excuses. He expects the same from his nomenklatura people. Thus the head of a factory, told by the province party chief to build byres for a herd of cows within three days for an important visit of inspection, did so without protest, complaint or request for help in the necessary wire-pulling, despite the effect on his production plan, for which he would have to answer to his ministry. This is the proper nomenklatura mode of operation, whatever pressure, threats, bullying and panic it may bring to the people below the man who gets the job done. Such a man might well be transferred to party officialdom, and make his way up that ladder, expecting the same from his nomenklatura and party subordinates, and getting done whatever his party superiors at the higher level might want, without complaint or excuses.

This is the schooling of party officials. It is still the main factor in the way the country is run, though it is beginning to break down. The men now at the top of the party pyramid received this schooling under Stalin, who was the apex of the pyramid. Since his death the number of highly trained and professionally experienced people in all branches of the administration, economy and cultural life has increased very greatly. They do not find it easy to be at the beck and call of party officials who may make ridiculous demands to no useful purpose and without understanding the problems involved. This kind of friction is becoming an important element in Soviet life. Factory managers and senior engineers, for example, are ceasing to be people of the traditional bullying nomenklatura type. Their party membership is, for many, of much less importance than their technical and professional work, though they have to be in the party because they hold responsible posts. They are *necessary* people—necessary in the sense that there must be such people in any developed country to run the economy, administration and public services. The party officials are necessary only in the sense that they form the present power structure of their country, from the top down to each locality, and nobody knows how to change the situation so that they do not get in the way of the people who actually run things.

This problem is most obviously acute in production. A Soviet engineer told the writer that production in his factory would stop if he and his colleagues did not lie awake at night working out ways of getting round the oafish interference by party and nomenklatura officials. The central party leaders have for many years now demanded that the local party officials must only supervise industry and not try to run it, but neither the leaders nor anybody else know what this means. Party intervention is usually essential, because of overall shortages. For example, the party leaders of a large industrial town in Siberia, where new factories and population growth had outrun the water supply, met daily to decide which factories and areas should be cut off. The town soviet, which is the local government authority, had quite inadequate status for such decisions. (The nomenklatura rank of the heads of a town soviet is usually lower than that of the heads of the big factories in the town.) So long as Soviet economic growth is overstrained, leading to shortages of this kind, there is some need for an indisputable authority in every area.

Indeed, so much of the energies of party bureaus is spent in helping factories to obtain scarce supplies or ensuring that farms fulfil the planned deliveries, and settling a great variety of practical matters of this kind, in an economy where acute emergencies are endemic, that the central party leaders are always worried at the insufficient attention of the local bureaus to overall *political* leadership, including in ideological matters. In 1962 the local party bureaus were divided into one for industry and one for agriculture in each area. (Local government being an important channel of party rule, the province and county soviets were similarly divided.) The purpose was to facilitate the party's supervision and intervention, but this raised more problems than it solved, and was abandoned together with Khrushchev, its instigator, two years later. One of the

Mass meeting at a factory

jokes at the time was that the English had decided to have two queens, one for industry and one for agriculture.

The life of ordinary people, who are not in charge of factories or institutions, is affected no less deeply by the existence of the pyramid of party officialdom and the associated nomenklatura system. Bullying by petty officials, who must be obeyed and not answered back, is an old part of Russian life. Its accentuation in the Stalin period was accepted, since people felt lucky merely to keep out of trouble with the political police and make a living, however poor. The bullying became worse after the war, partly because of the strain of war and partly because of the consolidation of party officialdom, which tends to set the tone and colour to all officials, however minor. Since then, what has been called the sergeant-major aspect of Soviet life has remained in force while material conditions have improved and fear of the political police has declined, and it has therefore become more important in people's minds. Minor mitigations were made around 1960; for example, some order was brought into the extraordinary

profusion of misdemeanours for which officials could fine their subordinates or members of the public on the spot.

To gain some impression of what might be uppermost in public opinion the writer brought up the word *spravedlivost* (fairness, justice) in casual conversations in Russia a few years ago. On the first occasion he was chatting with a lady barber who was shaving him. On hearing that 'maybe a little more spravedlivost might not come amiss', she became so excited, with the open razor in her hand, that for an instant the situation seemed perilous, but the remark had caught her sympathy, not resentment, and she told a long story of unfair treatment in respect of wages without effective means of redress. This lady, and many other people subsequently, strongly reinforced the writer's surmise that this word was one of the keys to the thoughts of ordinary people. The lack of a democratic tone of life at the lowest levels is, in the opinion of Soviet people with whom the writer has been able to discuss this highly political question, due to the nature of the party, its organisation and its attitudes, rather than

Delight at a space success

to the lack of any alternative party. By the party they mean, not the 13 million members, but the 200,000–300,000 party bosses and their immediate lieutenants, known in Russia as the *apparat*—mainly the local bureaus and their senior staffs—who are responsible not only for controlling the ordinary members but, through the nomenklatura members, who number several million, for the whole of public life in their areas.

Up to the early 1930s, when there was still a good deal of faith in the party in the Russian towns, many people joined it out of conviction. This does not happen now. New members are invited to join because they are influential amongst their workmates or, more usually, because their jobs carry rather more responsibility than most, such as skilled work at key points in the production process, or quality control, or work as a foreman, or as a section manager in a collective farm, or in charge of, say, a dozen clerks in an office. It is possible to resist the invitation, but only with the aid of excuses and not always for long. It is not normally possible for a person without specialist education to get such a job without joining. It is embarrassing for ordinary workers to join because their workmates conclude that such a man is on the make, climbing up towards 'them'. Disinclination to join is probably growing amongst professional people, but since they are often in positions of administrative responsibility they find membership difficult to avoid. Scientists can and do refuse.

At one time in the early 1960s, when the zigzag of 'de-Stalinisation' was at a relatively democratic turn, it was decided to allow secret voting in electing the secretaries of primary party groups. These are not regarded as within the apparat: they are the lowest level of party officialdom; the primary groups are usually at the place of work and the secretary is not supposed to receive time off his job or any payment for this function, unless the group is unusually large. Thus the experiment was in fact a very mild one. But it was not a success. The party magazine, after making it clear to rank-and-file members that they had the right to vote in secret, a few months later began referring to 'knights of the pencil'—i.e. those who preferred ballot-papers to a show of hands, for the apparat officials were finding that too many of their nominees were being turned down. There has never, since the present political structure was developed early in the Stalin period, been the slightest question of the party bureaus being in any way subject to effective election. In 1961 it was decided that members of the bureaus, at all levels from county to the Politbureau in Moscow, should not serve for more than a certain period (except for Khrushchev himself and a few others), but this provision was never put into effective practice. The apparat men simply moved from one province, town or county to another, and the rule was dropped in 1966.

Another attempt by the party leaders in recent years to do something about the increasing rigidity of the political system in face of the growing need for flexibility has been to move people more often between the party apparat on the one hand and the civil service and business management of the same area on the other hand. In practice, since the apparat men usually have not the necessary skills for normal administration and management nowadays, this often amounts to moving 'practical' people into the apparat. There has always been some movement between the 'practicals' and the apparat, but the two kinds of work have tended to attract increasingly different kinds of people in recent years. The apparat shows a very marked preference for recruiting into its junior ranks young men of its own kind who do not like to think for themselves and do like to tell other people what to do and think, while unquestioningly accepting the views and instructions of their own superiors in the apparat. In technical

The factory dinner-break

colleges and universities it is quite easy to pick out the small minority of students who are aiming at a career in the apparat, and the majority, who are usually more successful in their studies and of better character, who will go into research, business management, technology, teaching, etc.

CENTRAL AND LOCAL GOVERNMENT

The political structure of the state, as distinct from the party, need not detain us long, despite its constitutional complexity, for it is of relatively little actual importance. The government of the USSR is formally appointed by the Supreme Soviet, but its senior members, such as the Prime Minister and his top Cabinet colleagues, are always Politbureau members. Below them are some 'overlord' ministers who are usually members of the Central Committee. The majority of ministers, of whom about 47 are each responsible for the administration of a particular industry, are more like the heads of the appropriate branches of the civil service than politicians. The economic ministers mostly know their industry well from experience in it; they and their posts constitute a kind of highest level of nomenklatura for the economy. The 15 Union Republics and the 20 Autonomous Republics each have their own Supreme Soviet and government. The several hundred ministers in all these governments are mostly, in effect, the most senior civil servants of the republics, implementing decisions reached by the republic party leaders, who themselves implement the decisions of the USSR Politbureau. The provinces, towns, counties and rural areas are administered by elected soviets, but these elections are like those to the USSR Supreme Soviet, without choice of candidate.

People in the USSR have been for several years expecting some choice of candidate, or at least some kind of genuine public participation in the selection of candidates, but the real selection of the single candidate for each constituency continues to be made by the local party authority, along the lines of the plan laid down by its superiors for the proportion of occupations, sexes, age-groups, party and non-party, and nationalities in the particular soviet. The most recent local elections showed the accustomed dispiriting methods: trade union and general public meetings were convened to nominate the candidates. This was followed by a delegate meeting to select the one decided from the outset by the party authorities. A smudgy leaflet containing his or her photograph and purely conventional brief election address was issued, followed by the formality of the public election. The newly elected soviet then proceeded to the formality of electing its executive committee, consisting of people on the local nomenklatura. There is an old Russian tradition of the public giving instructions to its representative, and this plays some part in Soviet elections: a list of local improvements that ought to be attended to is usually put forward at the meetings which nominate the candidate. This list is to a great, but not necessarily complete, extent a formal one, drawn up or agreed beforehand by the local party leaders.

Elections are fairly frequent. Those to the local soviets (province, town, town ward, county and rural soviets) take place every second year, usually in March. The proportion of the electorate voting in the local elections has usually not reached the virtually 100-per-cent levels for the Supreme Soviets, and there have been cases of a re-election being necessary at the rural level because a candidate has not received the statutory minimum of half the possible votes. However in the 1967 local elections, an average of 99·94 per cent voted, and of these an average of 99·7 per cent voted for the candidate. Membership of a soviet, except rural soviets, is generally regarded as a mark of distinction, for the person concerned has been chosen by the party to become a member and some small influence attaches to the office. Among the writer's Russian acquaintances are two sisters, one a forewoman and the other in charge of a small factory office in the same provincial town. One was invited to join the party and the other to become a member of the town soviet, at about the same time. Both invitations came through the party organisation. They accepted. Membership of the soviet took up more time than that of the party. The soviet member was offered a bribe by a local state trading organisation to exert her influence on its behalf. This would not happen to the party member, as she would not have sufficient influence in that capacity.

ECONOMIC ADMINISTRATION

The economic framework of Soviet life follows the pattern of political organisation. All industry, transport and wholesale trade, most of retail trade and about half of agriculture is owned by the state and is administered by the economic members of the USSR government. All state enterprises in the most important branches, such as the various defence, fuel and power industries, iron and steel, other metals, the more important branches of engineering, construction and transport are directly controlled by their central ministries. For other branches, such as agriculture, food-processing, textiles and trade, there are ministries in the Union Republics, which either run the smaller enterprises on their territory, leaving the larger ones to the central ministries, or

This Baku girl has joined the Young Communist League, but still attends the Palace of Pioneers, wearing her Pioneer neckcloth, to continue with carpet weaving

run them all, under the general direction and coordination of central government authorities. The parts of agriculture and trade which are not state-owned are the cooperative enterprises, principally the collective farms, as co-operatives of producers, and the rural shops, as consumer cooperatives. In practice, however, the latter, which are of minor importance since there is relatively little trade in the villages and the villagers do not regard the shops as in any sense their own, are officially treated as part of state retail trade. The collective farms are subject to a great deal

Announcing Socialist competition between two factories

of control by the local offices of the Ministry of Agriculture, and even more directly by the county party bureaus. Thus, in effect, the entire economy may be regarded as state-owned or controlled, with one important exception—the household allotments in the villages, which the collective farmers regard as their own, and which they are free to cultivate as they please, within certain limits.

For practical economic purposes the key territorial units are the provinces of the large republics, the small republics and the largest towns. Thirty or 40 different ministries may be in charge of the enterprises in one such area. It is the function of the managers of these enterprises to fulfil the production plans set by their ministries, assuming that the planned supplies arranged by their ministries, with the help of the USSR State Planning Committee in Moscow, arrive on time, or arrive at all. As noted earlier in this chapter, there are always crises and emergencies, and some local coordinating authority, powerful enough to override a distant ministry if necessary, and to arrange emergency measures, is essential. This is the economic function of the party bureau in such an area, but there has always been some disinclination amongst party leaders in Moscow to recognise this fact, though they are keenly aware of it; most of them have been province First Secretaries themselves. Ideally, the party's function in production is to inspire and enthuse the masses and the specialists, to make them aware of the world-political and patriotic importance of good work, and to make sure that the most loyal and competent men are the managers. It should not be necessary to intervene in matters for which the ministries and their local offices and the central and local planning bodies exist. Continuous party intervention is a sign of defeat in the problem of organising the socialist economy. In 1957 an attempt was made to meet this problem by abolishing the central economic ministries and putting all the industry of each province and small republic under a local economic authority with greatly strengthened powers for local planning. However, central ministries almost immediately reappeared under other labels, and in 1965 the local economic councils were abolished and central ministries were re-established as such, but the republic governments were given more industrial authority in an effort to retain some of the advantages of decentralisation.

The problem is, in effect, one of super-large organisation. The whole country is one gigantic firm, owned in theory by the state on behalf of all the citizens and administered by their government. (In practice, it would be nearer the facts of the situation to say that it was owned by the party apparat, because its members make or control all the really important economic decisions at all levels—though this is not the case in any legal sense.) No way has yet been found of running so colossal an organisation without the apparat, itself organised in a kind of military hierarchy, stepping most actively into the breach at every level. But the number and complexity of industrial enterprises, and the intricacy of their interdependence in the modern conditions of technical specialisation, are increasing all the time. The ministries, planners and local party authorities are finding it increasingly difficult to cope. There is no solution in sight, other than freedom for the managers to act more like their counterparts in the market economies, with the right to make their own decisions, whether on the criterion of profit or on some other criterion which has not yet been invented. There are very great difficulties in the way of such a solution, but some changes in this direction were made in 1965, at the same time as the ministries were re-established.

All developed countries, irrespective of whether they are socialist or capitalist, are finding that the quality of life is coming to be influenced by the problems of administration. This is true to a far greater extent for citizens of the USSR because so much more of the country's life is administered. There is a general sense of great changes being essential in the political and economic structure and in the manner of its administration, but there is no possibility as yet of open discussion of this problem, except for certain permitted aspects of limited importance. The aspect on which most public attention is centred at present is whether and to what extent industrial managers should be allowed to choose their suppliers and customers, to engage and dismiss labour, to negotiate wages and the prices of their products and to decide what to produce.

3

Life in the Villages

THE BACKGROUND

Five-sixths of the Soviet population live in the great plain which comprises the European part and in the long strip of Southern Siberia. The other sixth mostly occupies the scrub or irrigated lands of Central Asia and the mountainous Caucasus. The entire population lives in a climate of temperature extremes. Even the most southerly areas are little above freezing-point in a normal winter and even the most northerly inhabitants enjoy a warm if brief summer. For the great majority of the people, the normal winter temperature is well below freezing-point and far below in Siberia. In the several break-downs which the country has suffered during this century, lack of fuel for heating has been almost as disastrous as lack of food. Nearly half of the country, mainly in the north and east, has 'permafrost', i.e. the subsoil is permanently frozen at various depths, which makes both agriculture and town-building difficult.

In the main farming area (European Russia and the Ukraine), moisture is sufficient only in the north but the soil is poor there, while the south has good soil but precipitation is just sufficient in a normal year. The paths of the *sukhovyei*, tongues of hot, dry winds from the Central Asian deserts, can be seen as well as felt in the East Ukrainian villages as the standing crops turn black under them. One of the winter activities of farmers is to make reed matting to cover the snow in order to slow down its rate of melting in the spring so that the moisture gets into the ground and does not wash the soil away. Gully formation is widespread in towns and across roads as well as on farmed land, due to insufficient drainage; a quarter of the area of Volgograd and a tenth of Novosibirsk are occupied by gullies and ravines. All villages near railways have a legal obligation to clear snow from the lines as required. Although only a tenth of the country's area is suitable for farming, very great investments in

drainage, irrigation, roads, farm buildings, fertilisers, livestock improvement, suitable machinery, village housing and services are still necessary to make even this tenth reasonably productive.

Geography influences other aspects of village life, such as education: distance and weather cause great difficulty in school atten-

A 'telega' cart – a common form of farm transport

dance other than at the village primary schools, especially in spring and autumn when even within a village the children have to wade through mud. The immense problem of road-building in the countryside has not yet been seriously tackled. In winter, travel and transport are made relatively easy by the frozen snow; in the spring thaw and the autumn rains the unsurfaced roads become mud swamps and in summer the potholes and dust make them a trial of endurance. Villages differ greatly, even within the European part of the Russian Republic, from the small and very numerous ones in the central provinces which have not yet emerged from their traditional crowded poverty, or the equally crowded Volga provinces of unreliable rainfall, to the steppe provinces north of the Caucasus with good soil and enough moisture, where the villages are large and far apart and where the terrain is suitable for the vast fields and the big heavy machines that are favoured for all areas by the Soviet authorities. The irrigated lands of Central Asia have almost continuous small groups of peasant dwellings rather than villages as such.

When the first Russian census was taken in 1897, 106 million people lived in the villages and 18 million in the towns. The town population is now (1968) about 130 million, while the rural population is still, after some fluctuations, the same 106 million as 70 years ago and is slowly declining. Its natural increase is more than balanced by emigration to the towns, which would be a good deal larger if collective farmers, who with their families now form only half the rural population, were legally free to leave their farms. During the period in which the steadily increasing town population has made Russia the second greatest industrial and technological country in the world, the material condition of life in the villages has changed rather slowly. Nearly half the farming families still do not have electric light, and about two-thirds still bake their own bread and rely on their own cow for milk. Transport remains abominable. Farmers' houses are still built of logs or whitewashed clay and thatched roofs are common, as are planks beside and above the stove for sleeping. Piped water is very rare and drainage almost non-existent. Lavatories sometimes are nothing more than a heap of straw somewhere outside, but wooden booths are now common. Modernisation of living conditions is very uneven, even in the European part, as it depends on many factors in addition to climate, soil and terrain. Villages near enough to towns to sell some of their produce direct to the consumer have more money to spend and the town shops to spend it in. Most of the villages are too far from a town, or the transport is too difficult, to enjoy this advantage.

The most important single cause of differences in rural prosperity is what might be called organisational luck. The collectivisation established, in the main, one farm for each village. When the turmoil it caused was over, by about 1935, some of the farms got off to a

A village street on a state farm

'Back Again' – a famous post-war painting, bold because its theme is unhappy and unheroic and thus not fully within Socialist Realism. But it was praised as 'condemning such fathers' and 'helping to strengthen our Soviet family life'

better start than others. The reason may have been that the change was managed relatively well by the party emissary sent from the town and morale was not destroyed nor many animals slaughtered, or that some of the more able and energetic peasants were not deported, or that the lack of a road limited the degree of control by the party authorities in the county town. In many of the villages there was support for a radical break with the past, especially amongst the young men, and in some this initial good will continued and helped to give the new system a foundation of willing effort. More important, perhaps, was the chance of a farm getting as chairman a particularly sensible and decent man with good connections, able to mitigate the demands made on it and to get supplies. By the time the war broke out, remarkable contrasts of extreme poverty and relative prosperity between neighbouring collective farms were common. By then, some were virtually independent, because they regularly fulfilled or exceeded their delivery quotas, which was all that the county party leaders were interested in, with enough horses and oxen to avoid dependence on the local machine-tractor station, enjoying well-organised handicraft, workshop and semi-legal commercial activities, with illegally large household plots, and able to afford the bribes necessary both to protect this independence and to get supplies. All this while adjacent farms remained utterly listless and dispirited, continually bullied by the county bureau, with a succession of chairmen from the dregs of the county nomenklatura. The latter kind of farm formed the vast majority.

During the war, at first things improved on both sides of the front line. Farms in the German-occupied areas began to disband, until the occupation authorities compelled them to retain, in principle, the Soviet form of organisation because it enabled agricultural supplies to be extracted more easily. On the Soviet side of the line the authorities relaxed control over the size of the household plot, which was immensely more productive than the collectively worked fields, and the farmers were able to impose their own prices on townspeople. After the war the controls were reimposed. The wartime private profits of the farmers were reduced to a tenth by devaluing the cash which they had hoarded. In order to compel the farms to concentrate upon agriculture, side activities such as brickyards and organised handicrafts were forbidden; and in order to compel the farm members to concentrate on the collective work as distinct from their own plots, crushing taxes and compulsory deliveries were imposed on the private animals, orchards and crops, while every collective farmer had to put in a minimum number of effective days' work in each season on the collective crops and husbandry. The county bureaus competed with each other to exceed their delivery quotas of agricultural products and to get the sowing, harvesting, threshing, autumn ploughing and so forth done ahead of the dates set by the province bureaus. Investment in agriculture was completely inadequate, since little could be spared for it under a policy of concentrating resources on heavy industry and the armed forces. The labour situation in the collective farms was desperate: after the postwar demobilisation they had only eight million able-bodied men in place of the 17 million before the war. As during the war itself, the unskilled work depended largely on the women. This is still the case, because there are still about 50 per cent more women than men of middle age in the countryside, and young men manage to get away to the towns more easily than girls.

The great contrasts in the prosperity of the collective farms have been reduced over the past 10 years, mainly by amalgamating the better ones with their neighbours. Until the early 1960s it was still very important for some member of a collective farm family to 'marry money', i.e. somebody working for money wages, because most farmers were paid almost entirely in kind. Now this is no longer necessary, as the government has greatly increased the prices paid to the farms for their products and in turn the farms' payments to members are mainly in money. In 1955 the Politbureau decided to give the farms more power to control their own affairs, so long as the plan of state deliveries was met. The laws passed to this effect remained almost dead letters because the county party bureaus, under the pressure of their superiors at province level, have continued to intervene in farm affairs in order to ensure these deliveries. This is not the first time that decisions of the party at the top have been frustrated to some extent by the nature and habits of its own hierarchy lower down. Khrushchev candidly admitted this problem when he declared that he was afraid to set in motion a policy of persuading the collective farmers to sell their private cows to the farm, because this would snowball into a campaign of undesirable pressure by the local officials. (Such a campaign did indeed occur, amounting in some areas to confiscation, reversed only on Khrushchev's fall a few years later.)

The growth of collective farm output stimulated by 'monetisation' lasted only five years; it had stopped by 1958 and Khrushchev became desperate, for he had promised the town population a reasonable standard of food and the farms were still quite unable to supply this. In consultation with toadying agricultural experts he took many decisions, and pushed them through the Politbureau, on drastic alterations in crops, such as the widespread sowing of maize for fodder, which is suitable to only a few regions of the USSR, and abolition of fallowing, which is essential in the drier areas. These policies snowballed down the line of the party hierarchy. Farms were compelled to plough in normal crops and plant others quite

The peasants' household plots behind the hou

unsuitable. The result was a very low harvest in 1963. Since people could not now be allowed to die of starvation, as had happened in Stalin's time, large imports of grain from abroad had to be paid for; the consequent heavy drain on the carefully husbanded gold reserves was a severe lesson to the government.

In the early years of his power Khrushchev had brought nearly 100 million acres of unused marginal land under the plough, mainly in Southern Siberia and Kazakhstan, by sending there the new machinery intended for existing farm areas and, with it, hundreds of thousands of young men, mostly from the towns. This bold and expensive step greatly helped to increase food supplies for several years, thus bridging the dangerous gap after Stalin's death had caused people's expectations to rise, but the yield in part of these 'new lands' has now dwindled to almost nothing. The farms established there were not collectives but state farms, on the same general principles as factories. The state farms in the older agricultural areas were increased in number and enlarged, by making over to them the lands of many adjacent collective farms. The machine-tractor stations were abolished, their equipment was sold to the collective farms and their workers, who went with the machinery, became collective farmers, while retaining many of their rights as state employees, such as pensions, holidays and trade union membership.

At present there are about 12,000 state farms in the USSR, averaging

eyond them is the collective farm proper

70,000 acres, of which about a quarter is under crops, with 2,000 cattle and 600–700 workers. The number of collective farms is now 36,000; their area averages 15,000 acres, of which half is under crops, and their cattle about 1,600. Perhaps 300 or 400 acres of this crop land consists of the household plots of the collective farm members, who own some 600 of the cattle as their private property. The average number of families on a collective farm is about 420.

It should be remembered that these averages are for the largest country in the world. Behind the average figures lie great differences in natural conditions, national and local farming traditions, and in ways of coping with the organisation of farm work, within the general framework described in the next sections.

COLLECTIVE FARM CONDITIONS

Even where the state and collective farms are well below the average size the scale of farming is very large indeed. At the same time it is minute, as a large proportion of the food is still produced on the household plots. These are nothing more than large gardens, usually by the farmer's house or very near it, but the policy of discouraging them which was followed until late in 1964 included removal of these plots to considerable distances in some farms. The vital difference between the plots and the giant collective fields is that the farmers are free to grow what they please in the former, the work being done by the family itself, for its own needs. The plots have always been cultivated with great devotion and intensity, despite the lack of suitable implements for this tiny-scale farming. One cow is permitted, unlimited poultry, a sow and a certain numbers of calves and piglets up to certain ages. The average size of the plot is now about an acre, but there are various arrangements between farms and their members for pasturing and supply of fodder. In addition, part of the fodder intended for the collectively owned animals finds its way illegally to those privately owned. These plots produced about half the food in the USSR until the early 1950s and still provide over a quarter, mostly in meat, milk, potatoes, vegetables and eggs, although they account for only about two per cent of the cultivated area. (They even produce about 20 per cent of the national wool supply and a third of this is used by the farm families themselves.) About three-quarters of the food produced on these plots is eaten by the family; the remainder is sold, either to local non-farming families or in the collective farm markets which are important institutions in all the towns, and in which the collective farms as such also sell produce.

The food in these markets is usually dearer than in the state food shops, but it is usually much fresher and of better quality. The markets are administered by the town authorities, who imposed price limits in the early 1960s, but since the fall of Khrushchev their traditional freedom of price movements has been restored, in contrast with the universal fixed prices in the state food shops. The markets have the liveliness, competition and choice associated with markets anywhere. Visitors to the USSR may find it instructive to compare the price and quality of food in these markets with the state food shops. Big differences of price indicate a shortage, or particularly poor quality, in the local state shops. In Stalin's time the towns would have starved without these 'free markets', just as the farmers themselves would have perished without their private plots, which still remain an outstanding problem in both national politics and village life. The party regards work on the private plots as unsocialist and the peasants regard it as obviously essential. Workers on the state farms are also allowed plots of land, but these are smaller, and many families in the towns have allotments and even cows, but these are of minor importance as contributors to the market in food though they are important for the diet of the families which cultivate them.

In Stalin's time the collective farms were forbidden to enter into any kind of association with each other. This ban remained in force until a few years ago, when associations of neighbouring farms were permitted—and are now encouraged—to run tractor and transport depots, small power stations (which were never prohibited), brick-making and timber yards, building enterprises, food processing, old-age homes for their members, and so on. Their effect in the form of new farm buildings, schools, small hospitals, clubs and housing is becoming visible in many areas. Another important recent improvement is the statutory introduction in 1965 of old-age pensions, sickness and maternity benefits and holidays for collective farmers, the cost being borne mainly by the farms but partly by the state. The standard benefit is 12

Collective-farm market in the town of Rostov

rubles (worth about £3) a month for rank-and-file collective farmers. There is now (early 1968) talk of providing some means whereby a farm member can defend his rights against the farm chairman and officials, on the analogy of trade unions and the labour sessions of the people's courts for state workers, but nothing has yet been done in this connection.

A more important inferiority of collective farmers before the law is their lack of a 'passport'—the identity document which has to be produced to the militia (the ordinary police) when anybody stays away from home for over 24 hours. It is needed for many other purposes, such as receiving a parcel through the post. A Soviet citizen is frequently asked to show his passport and collective farmers have to make laborious special arrangements. Without this document, which is provided to urban citizens at the age of 16, members of collective farms must obtain certificates from the farm office and the local soviet if they wish to spend more than a night elsewhere. It is impossible to opt out of the farm without obtaining a passport.

Young men get one fairly easily when their army service is over—
which is why more boys than girls are able to leave the farms. It is
possible for a farm member to get a passport also by taking a con-
tractual period of service with a state organisation which has authority
to recruit labour from the farms for work such as lumbering; after the
three or more years of the contracted service, one is legally free not
to return to the farm. For older or physically weaker farm members
this is not easy, and the indignity of this situation is felt nowadays
more than in Stalin's day, when there were more loopholes because
the towns needed labour and controls were less efficient. (Farm
members normally have no difficulty in getting permission to leave
the farm in order to marry into another collective farm, with the
exception that a man may not move into Moscow province and
certain other areas for this purpose, though a woman may, because
villagers there have the same rights as townsmen to passports.) There
are other disparities in law, such as the law of inheritance, for the unit
of private property ownership in the farms (the house and its contents and the animals and crops on the household plot) is the household, in accordance with traditional peasant law in Russia, whereas
for all other citizens it is the individual. Farm families are a good deal
smaller than a generation ago, partly because each household has the
right to a plot, which stimulates families to split up more than they
would otherwise do.

In describing present-day life on a collective farm, all those
normally visited by foreigners must be regarded as unrepresentative.
There are a few such near each of those main towns which are open
to foreign visitors. These farms are genuinely prosperous, and though
they receive subsidies in various forms from the authorities when
placed on the tourist list, this eminence is not welcomed. Farms near
big towns which have been doing very well have been known to
hold back their progress deliberately, for fear of being put on the list,
which means that a special interest in their affairs will be taken by
the authorities and a stream of tourist groups and of delegations from
the other socialist countries will have to be entertained during the
busiest months. Such farms have abnormally good buildings,
prosperous and attractive small industries, and in some cases their
own shops for the sale of their products in the towns, while the road
from the town to the farm is usually good.

A collective farm is a cooperative undertaking, on land owned by
the state but leased for ever to the cooperative without payment. The
collective livestock, farm buildings, the products and nowadays most

A state stall in Samarkand

of the machinery are the collective property of the members. The farm is administered by its chairman, who is elected by the members. All this is the case in theory but not in practice. For example, in the early 1960s in some provinces many farms were changed by decision of the province party bureau from collective to state farms and then —when the Politbureau thought the process had gone too far—back into collective farms, without the wishes of the members being considered in either transformation. As for the farmers collectively owning the farm property, it would astonish everybody if a member, on leaving a farm, asked for his share. Nor are chairmen elected by the members in fact, though a vote is taken at a meeting of members: these elections have almost always been dominated by an emissary from the county bureau, if not the First Secretary himself, when there has been any possibility that his nominee might not be elected. All important decisions about the work of the farm and allocation of its profits between pay to members and farm improvements are supposed to be made by meetings of the members, whereas in practice any such matters which the county bureau considers may affect its own success in implementing its targets of agricultural deliveries are subject to its overriding control.

But, whatever the differences may be between theory and practice, now that the collective farms are so big there are tendencies towards greater independence in the management of their affairs, and in some ways such tendencies are being encouraged by national policy. For the same reason, however—the sheer size of the farms—it is difficult to get anything like full meetings of the members, who also find it hard to influence the internal bureaucratic administration. The bigger collective farms may stretch 10 miles or more, with extremely poor internal transport between the villages. Membership varies, in different parts of the country, from under 100 to several thousand. The chairman and his staff, with the help of an elected board, have to organise the work and pay of all these people in the collective fields, the livestock sub-farms and on the small-scale industrial work that is now developing in the farms. The organisation of work is based on villages, through brigade leaders who are in charge of up to 100 members or more.

The tendency nowadays is for the chairman to be a graduate in some branch of agriculture, brought in from the province capital and placed on the county party committee, not merely on the county nomenklatura. He is not easily accessible to ordinary farm members. Some of these new style chairmen live in the county towns and are driven in to their office on the farm each day. There are, however, still plenty of chairmen of peasant and local origin, in the smaller and the more remote farms. The brigade leaders and heads of livestock sections are local men, much closer to the members. Although the majority of the ordinary members, who do the field work and look after the animals, are women, almost all chairmen, the great majority of board members and brigade leaders and the large number of emissaries and inspectors from the party bureau and the government offices in the county town are men. Some farms, with almost no men amongst the ordinary workers other than the tractor-drivers and mechanics, give an impression of all the hand labour being done by women who are ordered about by men.

Almost all the farms now have enough people in the party to provide sizeable party groups. These consist mostly of the chairman and other administrators, most of the brigade leaders and some tractor-drivers. One or two of the village teachers may be in the party and these are likely to be women: in some places they are farm members, with their own cottage and plot of land. But even if technically employed at a salary by the county education department, the teachers are paid partly by the farm in house, plot and some food supplies and are not very different from farm members. The same is coming to be true of agricultural specialists on the farm, but a fully trained doctor, if there is one, is more likely to be a salaried woman or man paid by the local office of the Ministry of Health. There are usually several of these people with specialist training in the party group. The resident party organiser on the farm, who runs this group, is often free full-time for this work if the group is a large one, even though he may nominally be a farm member or a salaried specialist with a different specific job.

For the purposes of calculating the earnings of farm members the work is in effect divided into three kinds: administrative; 'mechanising' (driving tractors, harvesters or lorries, electrical work, repair and maintenance of machines); and 'horse-and-hand' work. The last is by far the most common, and there are farms where the only males doing it are some boys and old men. The total days of work done in a year by each member of the farm are recorded. The value of a day's work is very different in each division and is reckoned in 'labour days'. Work without machines, but which requires some experience—such as milking by hand—is usually reckoned to be worth one labour day per actual day's work, although it may be very arduous. The various kinds of horse-and-hand work range in value from about half to two labour days for each actual day's work, according to the skill and responsibility of the job. 'Mechanisers' earn up to four or five labour days for a day's work. For senior administrators it is higher, especially for the chairman. Thus a horse-and-hand women might work 150 actual days and earn about the same number of labour days, a mechaniser might work for 220 actual days and earn 800 labour days, a bookkeeper might earn the same for working nearly 300 actual days in the year, and the chairman a good deal more. At the end of the agricultural year, the number of labour days earned by all the members of a farm is added up and the total number is divided into the amount of money and produce available for paying them. Thus the value in cash and kind of a labour day has tended to be different every year and in every collective farm.

Average cash incomes from collective farm work in the Russian republic for the year 1964 for various grades were as follows: chairmen—2,223 rubles; brigade leaders—933; mechanisers—844; horse-and-hand workers—346. For a day's actual work the chairmen received on average seven rubles 22 kopeks, the brigade leaders three rubles, the mechanisers three rubles 83 kopeks and the horse-and-hand workers one ruble 79 kopeks. There has been a steep rise in

The chairman of a collective farm and its best members (Byelorussia).
Left to right: *tractor driver, 'honoured collective farmer', chairman,*
brigade leader, milkmaid, brigade leader

collective farm earnings since 1964—possibly 40 per cent. (The purchasing power of a ruble may be taken as between four and five shillings.)

The idea of the labour day still has a bad connotation in the countryside because of its very low value until about 10 years ago. On many farms it was literally valueless in Stalin's time, as there was no surplus to divide amongst the members. In the great majority of farms it was worth a few pounds of grain—for bread and fodder for the cow—and either no money at all or extremely little. Until 1958 the mechanisers received wages, not labour days, as they worked for the state in the machine-tractor stations; when these were disbanded in 1958 and the machines sold to the collective farms, these men became farm members, but had to be paid at about the same level as their previous wages, so their labour day equivalents were, and remain, very high. They also kept their pension, sickness pay and holiday rights, which aroused jealousy in other farm members who did get them, on a more modest scale, seven years later. There is much talk at present of replacing the labour day by a wages system. The difficulty is that, in theory, the members of a collective farm are paying themselves out of the collective profits, which cannot be known in advance. In practice, there have usually been advance payments, unless the members could expect nothing and were living entirely off their household plots and pilfered collective property. Something like a wages system is now emerging. In the last few years, with all farms anticipating a profit, a system of guaranteed advance payments has been introduced. In about a third of the farms this is now paid entirely in cash, the members buying the food and fodder not grown on their plots from the farm or the village shop, which is not necessarily advantageous. Most farms now pay their members mainly in money and partly in kind. In 1966 the central authorities recommended to the collective farms that something like a minimum annual income in cash, or in cash and kind, should be guaranteed. In 1967 this was extended to regular fortnightly guaranteed payments (state wages are paid

A collective farmer and her house near Moscow

fortnightly). The recommendations were backed up by permission for the farms to obtain bank loans for the purpose.

The members of collective farms which have been incorporated in state farms now receive wages as employees of the state. It is, however, not easy for the state to take over all the collective farms in this manner, because it would saddle itself with responsibility for paying wages to their approximately 30 million remaining members, whatever the level of the harvest. Moreover, it is not possible to abolish or greatly reduce the household plots, from which collective farmers, on average, still get about 40 per cent of their food and money. Much of their time is spent by households on their own plot and the sale of its produce. Such concentration of effort on the family plot could not be allowed in a state farm, run on lines akin to industry. The collective farms, in effect, are a kind of compromise between the old peasant family farm (which was 10–20 times the size of the present plot) and the state farming system. It is uncertain whether collective farming can ever recover from the fact that it is a cooperative system in name only, having been imposed by force and mercilessly exploited by the state for a generation, during which the extent of detailed control by local party officials who were not interested in farming as such, and who still control the farms, has destroyed the interest and initiative of the farmers in anything other than their own tiny plots. A Soviet agricultural scientist remarked recently that the Russian peasant has lost his sense of the land except on the scale of a third of a hectare. Now that industrial growth both enables the Soviet state to put substantial resources into the land and is compelling it to provide the towns with a decent standard of food, the future of the collective farm system is one of the big question-marks in the USSR. A committee for drafting a new collective farm statute, to replace the 1935 one, has been sitting for many years and it is now said that the task has been indefinitely postponed.

GLIMPSES OF VILLAGE LIFE

In the present period of change and doubt, conditions vary even more than usual in different parts of the USSR. It would not be possible to give an accurate description that would fit the whole country, even if the main facts were known—which is very far from the case. Here are some first-hand accounts and opinions, mostly from people who have lived all their lives or many years in the areas concerned. The dates are important because of the speed at which conditions may be changing. Only the 1968 item, on p. 72, is up to date and a direct experience of the author.

Southern Ukraine, 1964; 'In the autumn the beets are transported to a government depot 26 kilometres away. Each brigade has to do its own loading of the beets into lorries, transport it to the depot and unload it there. All the brigades consist of women. Usually it is already icy cold, yet the women have to ride in open lorries in wind and rain, some without shoes and stockings. Social life is pretty dismal. There is a farm club with a leaking roof and two fly-spotted portraits, of Lenin and Khrushchev. The mobile cinema unit comes once in about two months. On May Day and 7 November the young folk may have a dance in the club, to the music of an accordion. Discontent amongst the collective farmers is great, especially when their bit of land with which they have managed to feed their families is taken away. They curse their lives. They say that life was better in the German occupation. Starting this spring, the size of the private plots has been further reduced and this gives rise to tears and lamentations.' (The private plot has been left alone since Khrushchev fell in October 1964.)

A relative of this informant who had lived abroad was repeatedly taken into the province capital for interrogation after saying at a farm meeting that in no capitalist country were people treated so badly as in the USSR. This man later committed suicide. The village had no electricity. A chimney for the lamp could be obtained only in the province capital. There was virtually nothing in nearer shops. The labour day for the poor harvest year of 1963 was half a kilogram of grain and some beets for the family and the cow, but no money.

В РАЙМАГЕ

— Селедкой торгую, овощ
ми. А теперь вот еще на кни
посадили...

Рисунок А. ЦВЕТК

North Caucasus, 1965;
People might easily die of
starvation, if not for their
plots, while waiting for their
farm pay to come through.
The situation deteriorated
after cessation of payment
in kind. Money pay now
reaches the farm members
late, sometimes several
months late, as the bank
first verifies completion of
the farm's task and only
then does it release the
money.

1965 (area not stated);
Household plots up to a
hectare are now allowed,
with no limit on the number
of animals and no taxes in
kind. Summer grazing is
provided by the farms, but no other fodder.

A country shop: herring, vegetables and plenty of books

Some counties not far from Moscow, 1965; After Khrushchev's fall,
the collective farms began leasing plots of two or three hectares, on
contracts for two years, the farm providing fertiliser, equipment and
transport. No controls, supervision or taxation. The lessee undertakes
to sell 60 per cent of his produce to the farm, at state procurement
prices, keeping 40 per cent for himself. The legal position is membership of the farm.

In Moldavia, 1960–6; Two large collective farms with fairly
young populations of 8,000 and 9,000 respectively, one Moldavian and
the other Russian. Members cannot get passports enabling them to
move elsewhere, even after military service. Russians travel to
Leningrad (1,000 miles away) to sell their own vegetables. But the
Moldavians work harder and earn more. Much drunkenness in both,
on illicit vodka. Nobody works on religious holidays, whether
believers or not. There is no national antagonism between these
adjacent farms.

In the Pripet Marshes, 1963;   This was never an easy farming area, but the peasants now say they greased their cart-wheels with butter before the war and are now slaves to the Communists. Party bosses are gods. An old woman is digging potatoes on her plot. A farm boss crushes her basket with his boot and beats her with a stick, as she screams, driving her to work in the fields. A local party boss sees a pretty young woman doing field work and asks her to spend the night with him. She is not in a position to refuse. The pay for a labour day is 'two cups of chaff'. Seven hundred of the 1,000 working farm members in this village are women. Household plots provide 80 per cent of the living. The state farms in the area are worse—one has to pay for wood, hay and use of pasture. Peasants live better near the big towns. (Comment: this part of the Pripet area was in Poland before the war. The conditions described may be due in part to the relatively recent collectivisation and in part to stricter control over formerly foreign territory; also possibly to the geographically isolated nature of the area.)

1963;   An Indian agricultural student managed to visit an ordinary collective farm. He saw three or four men riding on horseback and shouting. It was explained that they were preventing members from pilfering.

Early 1960s;   Some members of a collective farm stood watching a hayrick burning. Asked why they were not trying to save it, they replied: 'Why should we? If they've got no hay, they'll give us back our cows.'

Novgorod province;   A Leningrad worker with wife and three children, earning 80 rubles a month and living in one room of 12 square metres, helped in his parents' collective farm in 1965. He thought his own conditions excellent in comparison with theirs. He gave his father 13 rubles—all the money he received for 45 days' work on the farm. The compulsory purchase of expensive and inefficient machinery allocated to the farm had greatly increased its cost of producing flax, which was double the price paid to the farm by the state for the flax. These machines were regarded as having lowered the standard of living in the villages of the province. The farms were better off when the work was done by hand. 'Poverty, filth, ignorance and bitterness' is his view of farm life.

1965;   A government finance official said a Western accountant would have a fit if he saw how collective farm accounts were kept. The aim of the chief bookkeeper was to keep the chairman off the hook concerning plan fulfilment.

Kursk province, 1964; There are five or six radio sets in each village. Information from foreign broadcasts is quickly shared and is believed more than Soviet sources. Resentment at Soviet economic aid to other countries is strong and is expressed openly at meetings.

Tatar Republic, 1964; Now life is quite good in the villages because the state farm and collective farm leaders are competent.

Stavropol province (North Caucasus); Potatoes fetched 50 kopeks per kilo in the market when the price in state shops was 13 kopeks, but the shops had no potatoes. Everybody blames the shortages on export of grain to the Africans and Cubans. The peasants are eating better than the towns. They say: 'The labour day belongs to the state but the labour night to us.'

Near Tashkent; The 'Yakov Sverdlov' show collective farm has a permanent guide staff for foreign groups, who are taken by a circuitous route from the city to miss the ordinary farms.

1965; During the past two years the collective farmers, usually regarded as the least politically aware or organised section of the

The accountant's office of a collective farm near Moscow

population, have displayed staggering solidarity when pressure was exerted on their household plots, and in protest against absurd policies enforced from outside.

Minsk province, 1956–64;   An Argentinian, repatriated after eight years on a collective farm, said he lived in a hovel with a leaking roof and earth floor. He collected dry leaves to keep the stove going. The farm had a club, but it was always closed. No books were available. His wife was expected to work despite her baby. As a tractor-driver he had to account for every drop of fuel—otherwise it was deducted from his pay. The machines were always being repaired.

1963;   The following is typical of ironic comment on agriculture heard in the villages and the towns. A county bureau agenda: 1. Building cowsheds; 2. Building Communism. There are no nails, so let us proceed to item 2.

Moldavia, 1968;   A collective farm visited by the author in August 1968 convinced him that in that area at least (known for its grapes and early fruit and vegetables as 'the garden of the USSR') a viable combination of collective and private farming is becoming possible. 'Horse-and-hand' members were earning 60–90 rubles a month from the collective work. Members were selling up to two tons of grapes in Kishinev market from their private plots at 80 kopeks to one ruble a kilo. The extent of improvements on this farm since the fall of Khrushchev (in the level of state prices for early fruit and vegetables, and the blind eye turned by the authorities on the size and number of private plots) gave an impression that—in this area at least—there had been something like a victory by the peasants over the party, made possible by the urgent need to improve the element of fresh vitamins in the food supply of the towns.

Early 1960s;   A foreigner of long residence in Moscow describes the prospects of boys living in a village 30 miles away which she frequently visited. They did not belong to a collective or state farm.

> Sixteen-year-old Sashka lives in a village near Nikulina Gora, the dacha settlement of the leading cultural lights. His ambition to become a lathe operator or a fitter seemed to be unrealisable. Where could he learn? Since his village has neither a rail nor bus connection (a regular bus service is run in summer only from Uspenskoye, 15 kilometres away), the only way out of the situation was to apply for a place in the hostel of a school for working youth

in Moscow. Sashka had little hope. The others in the village laughed at him: 'Who's going to take you, a village boy?' He repeated his application three years in succession. To the surprise of the villagers he even received a reply: 'No vacancies.' Sashka had no desire to work on the local collective farm, which would mean an hour's walk. Apart from the chairman, the veterinary surgeon who made occasional calls and the party organiser, he would have been the only male person there, since all men capable of work had hired themselves out as (for the most part) unskilled labourers in Moscow or Zvenigorod and elsewhere. Accordingly, he did odd jobs in his mother's house, chopped wood, gathered mushrooms and berries with the other villagers, carried drinking water with the other boys from the spinning mill, which lay some 40 minutes' walk away and which employed only women, and played football. He wanted to avoid for as long as possible buckling down to a job which did not interest him. That would have to come sooner or later. He was already thinking of hiring himself out as a labourer at one of the nearby construction sites.

Sashka's younger friend, Vitya, is short-sighted and squints. Although he is intelligent he has difficulty in keeping up with his lessons at the collective farm school, which is one hour's walk away. He is ambitious. At home his smaller brother has to read the lessons aloud for him. The village children's attitude to the school is: 'When it snows we don't go. Nobody goes. The teacher doesn't know anything anyway. Would they have sent her to a farm school otherwise? Even if we learn something we won't get anywhere anyway.' When the dirt roads have been softened by rain or thaw, the boys still don't go to school. Their parents sleep when it rains. This village is typical.

Vitya would like to get an education so that he can later join a profession of his own choice, leave the village (which he nevertheless loves and defends proudly) and be like those people whom he knows only from seeing them on the farm's television set. One of the factors which will decide his future is the pair of spectacles which he may never acquire, since (as they told his mother in the Zvenigorod clinic) he would have to go to Moscow for them. In Zvenigorod no one bothers much about 'country bumpkins'. So far the transfer of Vitya's case has been tied up by the voluminous red tape of the Zvenigorod hospital. No clinic in Moscow is responsible for such cases. Furthermore, Vitya's mother works at the spinning mill and has to look after the hut, the cow and the smaller children. The 25 kilometres to Zvenigorod represents a problem from the point of view of time, money and transport. It takes a lot of visits to a clinic to get a hearing. And then there is the trip to Moscow, which is twice as far away. And then there are the smaller problems like what to wear and how to behave in the big city.

STATE FARMS

The differences between collective and state farms are now much less than a few years ago. Both kinds of farm are very large and usually consist of several big units, each based on a village or group of villages and each under a (collective) brigade leader or a (state) sub-manager. In both kinds of farm there are the same four social and economic classes: the administrators; the rural specialists such as vets, teachers and doctors; the mechanisers; and the horse-and-hand workers. In the state farms more of the work is done by machinery, there are many more men amongst the horse-and-hand workers, and more of the latter are party members. The housing and amenities are better because it is easier to get building materials, family life is more complete because there are more men, and there is more money around because regular money wages are paid, as in a factory. The biggest difference is probably still the amount earned, but the income gap is narrowing. The fortnightly advance payments on labour-day earnings of collective farmers are now intended by the government to be analogous to wages, at the same rates of pay as state farm wages. However, since there is little farm work to be done in winter, the collective farmers do not get this pay all the year round, but this is being remedied by the new freedom of their chairmen to set up small industrial enterprises. The most important social difference is the possession of a passport in most cases by the state-farm worker, which means no legal obstacle in leaving the farm, though he cannot just go to a town for work: like any other passport holder, he has to be 'written in' by the town militia, who will do so only if he has a job there, and he may have to go further afield if the province party authorities forbid the employment of people from state farms which may be short of labour. However, the possession of a passport does mean full citizenship status.

The schools and medical facilities in state-farm villages are fully provided by the state and therefore usually better than in the collective farms, and the children in a good state farm have more chance of going on to secondary or technical school. The state farm worker, being a wage-earner, has a trade union and a fixed working day. In practice, these advantages may not amount to much. For example, overtime is limited by law and is allowed only with the union's agreement, but if the farm management insists, much illegal overtime will be worked, and without overtime pay if it is not provided for in the plan. But the collective farmers are much worse off: they are expected to work 'from

A modern poultry farm in the Crimea

dawn to dawn' at harvest time (just when they need to spend most time on the household plot): there is no legal limit to their hours, nor days off at weekends; working time in practice depends on the ability of the chairman or brigade leader to bully or persuade, as longer hours may bring no extra earnings.

In most collective farms the members do have more independence than their counterparts in the state farms: they are nearer to the original peasant condition, treating their household plots and livestock as their own miniature farms. However, such satisfaction as there may be in working for oneself should not be overestimated in the case of the collective farm member, for most of the work on the household plots is done by the women who would be only too glad not to have to do it; in any case tenure is felt to be precarious, for a turn of the invisible political wheel in Moscow may at any time bring another squeeze on this last legal bastion of independence and private enterprise. The state-farm workers have cut their link with the old peasant condition. They are much nearer to the outlook of the townsman employed in a state factory.

The difference in conditions between state farms is not so great as those between collective farms, since the government has always been directly responsible for the former and has had to subsidise those that could not pay their way. Nevertheless, even for state-farm workers much has depended on the 'organisational luck' mentioned above in connection with the collectives, the main factor being the quality of management, in particular the capacity and desire of the manager to protect the interests of his workers and at the same time not to forfeit the confidence of the party and government authorities under whom he has to work. He is appointed by a ministry responsible for the state farms, through its republic or province offices, but is on the nomenklatura of the province party bureau, which is his real master.

A former Soviet citizen, who was the director of various state farms until 1960, told the writer that he had to be a tight-rope artiste, balancing between the needs of the soil, the demands of the party authorities, the good will of his workers and the constraints put by the law on his initiative as manager. This man always took care to have reliable friends in the province and republic party office; this enabled him to take more risks than would otherwise have been practicable in order to treat his workers well. For example, they were entitled to not more than 15-hundredths of a hectare for personal use: he allowed them extra plots in areas which inspectors were not likely

Board of Honour: state farm in Kazakhstan
(1965)

to visit. He was in moderate trouble with the financial authorities several times for overstepping his authority, but the party always supported him. Fluctuating policies enforced from Moscow on the size of state farms and in favour of some crops and against others had a deadly effect. He worked extremely hard and was regarded as a good farm manager by his superiors. In 1960 he had the opportunity to leave the USSR legally, for good. Although a firm patriot and a party member who, in principle, believed in the ultimate aims of Communism, he decided to live abroad because he was exhausted by the strain. Before making

Celebrating on a state farm in Kazakhstan (1965) – the people are mostly of German origin

this decision he visited various areas of the USSR where he could obtain a higher administrative position in agriculture, but decided that the same kind of strain would be unavoidable. (After informing his superiors that he had decided to emigrate, some attempt was made to commit him to an asylum, but he was able to avoid this. One of the things that saved him was the refusal of his staff to testify that he had behaved in a psychologically abnormal manner. An unpopular director would probably not have enjoyed this loyalty.) This man lived well as one of the local élite, having a car, horses and motor boat for his personal use. (However, he was subsequently able to run a much better car as an industrial worker in West Germany.) His experience of state farms occupied the decade of the 1950s, but his problems are still, in principle, the same for managers of state farms today. The most important difference is that the wages of the lowest-paid workers have been raised considerably since his time. Ways of allowing directors to exercise more initiative were being tried out in a few hundred state farms during 1968. These experiments are rather cautious, and for all the other state farms the plan targets received from above remain very detailed, expressed in over 50,000 specific figures each year for the crops, animals and every kind of activity. A director is legally bound to observe these innumerable instructions, although in practice it is impossible. Quite radical proposals are now being canvassed by some Soviet economists to give state farm directors genuine scope for initiative, based on the profit motive.

A young American student of Soviet agriculture was allowed to spend a month in 1960 on one of the most successful state farms in the USSR, which many foreigners have visited for a day. It is situated in the rich steppe land north of the Caucasus. The farm, with 1,500 workers and 26,000 acres of land under crops, was administered in five divisions, based on village settlements, the central village having a secondary school, cafeteria and recreation club in addition to the main offices and machinery depots. In rainy weather the internal road connecting the centres was impassable to lorries, jeeps or tractors. Food is sold at cost price to the workers, who thus fare far better than workers in Moscow, and live mostly in clean barracks, some in their own timber homes. Laundry is washed in the local stream and an outdoor water tap is available to each group of several families. Bicycles, radio sets, books and Czech motor cycles are in evidence. The farm manager works a 14-hour day and his immediate assistants and experts are competent, but the managers of the farm's territorial divisions and their assistants are much less effective, some being very incompetent. The attitude of the older workers to the manager was subservient, but in general, especially among war veterans and those working with machines, it was independent. Some of these had come to the farm from town jobs in search of peace and quiet.

The great disciplinary force on the farm was the wage system: pay, benefits such as sanatorium passes, and various privileges depend rigidly on the number of years in continuous employment and on job qualification. Field work done by hand, such as weeding, and the work with animals—which involves a 5 a.m. to 9 p.m. day—is done basically by women, prematurely aged and without husbands, who get the lowest pay. Educational opportunities are good because of the secondary school, many of the pupils who complete it being able to go on to intermediate or higher education, but those who leave school earlier find their prospects limited to the farm and they tend to behave badly. Sport is the chief organised distraction. The local political police kept careful watch on the farm for 'economic crime'. There were 300 party members on the farm, with one full-time party organiser. Political and production meetings were conventional and lifeless, with the striking exception of reaction amongst the women to the danger of war at a protest meeting on the incident of the American spy plane. Machinery was apt to be handled ignorantly and arrangements for repair were very inadequate, including a great dearth of small, simple tools. Despite the very special status of this farm, it was in need of great investments and much more competent management of the divisions. Each division is 10 times the size of American Mid-Western grain farms and productivity is nowhere near American standards.

The following are more recent indications of life on state farms in other parts of the country.

A cotton-growing state farm 50 miles from Tashkent, 1964; The workers are housed in communal blocks, one small room per family, without drainage or piped water. Only administrators, central office staff and specialists receive fixed pay. The workers receive two kopeks per kilogram of cotton picked and brought in. In order to prevent them leaving, permission was obtained from the Uzbekistan Cotton Board to pay four kopeks. During the day the living quarters are deserted: everybody, including children and the aged, is in the fields. Even at four kopeks it is necessary to work from 6 a.m. to 9 p.m. with one hour for lunch, for the families to make a living. They drink from irrigation ditches and dysentery is widespread. The authorities kidnapped people on the streets of Tashkent to help in the cotton picking.

A wine state farm in the Crimea, 1964; The workers earn about 20 rubles a month, but sell a good deal of pilfered grapes to visitors at local resorts and grow fruit on their allotments for sale. (The legal minimum wage was 40 rubles a month in 1964.)

1963; Some state farms are being changed into collective farms, as the management cannot meet their wage obligations. State farm workers steal from the farm on a very large scale—equipment and anything of value as well as food.

RURAL ADMINISTRATION

In addition to the management of the collective or state farm itself, the administrative factors influencing the lives of the farmers are local government and the local party authority. The latter is by far the more important and affects the farm directly, through its director or chairman, who has to spend much of his time in the province capital or county town at party meetings or reporting in detail to the bureau on his implementation of their instructions; through party emissaries from the county town who visit the farm frequently on tours of inspection; and through instructions to the group organiser of the party members on the farm. Province and county offices of the Ministry of Agriculture are of minor importance in comparison with the party offices as controlling and inspecting authorities.

As for local government, this has never been of much significance in the Soviet countryside. The real power in the villages until collectivisation was the *mir*, or commune, a traditional assembly of all heads of households. The party was in the 1920s extremely weak in the rural areas, and the rural soviets which had been set up after the civil war became, in effect, the stage on which the party fought unavailingly against the mir for influence amongst the peasantry. Collectivisation destroyed the mir. The rural soviets remained so weak that local government was undertaken directly by 'political departments' set up in the machine-tractor stations, which were in effect the armed centres of local power. In the mid-1930s local governmental authority was formally restored to the rural soviets but by then the party authorities in the county towns had been augmented sufficiently to take over effective control, which they still maintain.

In the past two or three years the Politbureau and government have issued several instructions and decrees aimed at strengthening the authority and importance of the rural soviets. Since these are elected by the local rural population as a whole, and the old village assembly or mir is not likely to revive, a genuine accession of authority by these soviets would be associated with a revival of the status and interests of the farming community and of rural life in general. (A large proportion of villagers are not directly engaged in farming, but this remains the predominant occupation, and the great majority of non-farming villages and villagers do not live very differently from the rank-and-file farmers.) Strong rural soviets could also act as a counter-weight against collective and state farm managements on behalf of the farmers. However, the rural soviets remain so weak that it was not until 1968 that they were authorised to have their own transport and to acquire materials with which to repair their premises. The functions of these soviets are mainly bureaucratic as the local organs

Picking cotton, near Tashkent

of the state. The chairman and secretary, and in larger ones also a finance officer, are paid for full-time service and run a small office in the central village of the area. They issue documents, such as birth, death, marriage and adoption certificates and application forms for passports, keep a register of men liable to military service, a register of households, have a legal responsibility for orphans, act as the local notary for contracts etc., keep a record of voters and of pensioners (the pensions are paid by the state farm or collective farm office), and have ill-defined duties in connection with local roads, schools and medical services, but virtually no resources. Their small income is mainly derived from a percentage on the income tax and on farm taxes. The state farm director or the collective farm chairman are far more important figures in the area than the chairman of the village soviet, because they control resources.

Another form of rural local organisation is the consumers' cooperative, which is supposed to run the village shop or shops. This has even less reality as a consumers' cooperative than the collective farm has as a producers' cooperative. Cooperatives were an important factor in many areas of the Russian countryside before the revolution. It is a tragedy that although in form they have been greatly expanded, in substance they have been virtually extinct since collectivisation.

Like local government, cooperation is not a channel of democracy in the USSR, and it would require a far-reaching change in the entire political structure and atmosphere for either form of representation to become alive. It is not likely that new life will be put into these dead bodies by decrees from Moscow or instructions down the party hierarchy to make them more active.

RURAL PROGRESS

Figures of 'sales in rural areas' published in December 1967 show impressive increases in annual sales of consumer durables from 1960 to 1966: the largest increases are in television sets—212,000 to 1,045,000; washing machines—55,000 to 878,000; refrigerators—45,000 to 311,000; vacuum cleaners—27,000 to 75,000. The poor quality of such goods does not diminish the rural revolution indicated by these figures, whether the goods are for private homes or village clubs. Sales of sewing machines, both in town and country, halved in the same period, in line with the tendency to buy more ready-made clothing.

There is more money around in the countryside than ever before. Some of the harvests since 1964 have been very good indeed by Russian standards, due to the stimulus of higher state prices for farm products and possibly to world-wide developments in agricultural science. The collective farms are using their new freedom to engage in non-agricultural enterprises to meet the keen demand for consumer goods in the villages and small towns as well as to provide building materials, farm buildings and houses for their own purposes. Their output is on a tiny scale compared with that of state industry, and depends on waste materials from factories and locally available materials, but they are now allowed far more freedom of initiative than factory managers, and may choose their suppliers and customers, what to produce and at what prices to sell, within rather broad limits. The plans they have to fulfil are deliveries of farm products to the state, now set for several years ahead, and they are otherwise now legally free to decide their own crops and herds. If the government does not withdraw these new rights and—more important—if the farms can escape the tutelage of the county party bureaus sufficiently to get chairmen with managerial and commercial flair, the countryside may revive and develop fairly quickly and even become, in a very small way, a spearhead of economic reform in the economy as a whole.

A new house on a collective farm. It is built in the traditional Russian style and is called an izba

The rural population came, in Khrushchev's time, to regard its conditions as intolerable, though there had been much improvement since Stalin. Khrushchev's successors have had to meet this mood by further increases in the state's procurement prices, much bigger investments in agriculture, social insurance and something akin to wages for the collective farmers and freedom for their household plots. To help overcome the acute shortage of goods in the country-side, now that the rural population has some money to spend, they have had to allocate more goods to rural areas and permit fairly free enterprise by the collective farms in non-agricultural activities. Thus the picture is an apparently inconsistent one, at what may be a historical moment of transition which is proceeding very unevenly in the various areas and aspects of rural life. Behind it all lies the mood of the towns, which must be met by better and cheaper food, amongst other things. Progress in rural life will not go far, however, unless the most competent and energetic young villagers remain—of their own free will—and the county and province party leaders and officials either change their nature or lose their power. Above all, farming and the farmers have to be recognised as constituting an interest in their own right rather than as a means of serving other interests. There is no sign yet that the central or local party leaders are capable of such recognition.

4

Life in the Towns

The development of material living conditions in the towns of the USSR from the 1890s, when industrialisation began, to the present time, has been broadly similar to that of the older industrial countries during their transition from farming to manufacturing. Effort has been concentrated upon the construction of an industrial economy and attention to conditions of life and work in the industrial centres has been delayed until the industrial economy has been firmly established. In the USSR serious concern for living conditions is still in its early stages. Because the economy is planned, material conditions can be improved drastically within a few years if the political authorities so decide, but it is unlikely that this will happen so long as the country holds to its world position as a super-power. The cost of the necessary arms and of associated activities, such as space exploration, is increasing all the time, while a high rate of industrial growth, which means investment in new factories for the purpose of making more factories rather than for making consumer goods, is also necessary to maintain this world position.

When in 1961 the political authorities announced the inception of Full Communism by 1980, they had no intention of making a big shift of resources towards consumption. They were guilty of a patently false promise made to allay public impatience for a better life, and to some extent of self-delusion: the figures of intended production for 1970 and 1980 which they issued at that time embodied the hope of industrial and agricultural output rising so fast that the standard of living could be made very high as a by-product, without diminishing relative military strength. In fact, the rate of industrial growth slackened off in the late 1950s and 1960s although it has recently recovered and in agriculture the recent improvement is far less than is needed to reach the targets for 1970 that were announced in 1961. Thus, the most likely trend is that living conditions will show a steady but not dramatic improvement. The conditions described in this chapter are likely to improve over the next few years, at about the same pace as the much higher standard of living in the older industrial countries will probably rise. The material standard of living in the larger Soviet towns is a half or less of that in Western Europe, and there is little prospect of this proportion changing greatly in the foreseeable future.

HOUSING AND SERVICES

The older towns of the USSR offer a picturesque variety to the eye, as is to be expected in a country which stretches across half of Europe and a third of Asia. Beauty, history and national character are there in plenty. The pleasure of foreign visitors who appreciate these things is also of course shared, in deeper measure, by the inhabitants. But, as in other industrial and industrialising countries, the great majority live in the more recent developments, which in the USSR comprise very many new towns and extensions of old ones built since the 1920s. Something like 100 million of the nearly 130 million townspeople live in urban developments of the last 40 years. For most of this period, until 10 years ago, construction was concentrated upon new mines, factories, steelworks, power stations, military installations, railways and administrative buildings. Schools, colleges and hospitals were given a lower priority, while housing, shops, restaurants, cinemas, laundries, domestic water and drainage and passenger transport came lowest on the list. The industrialisation involved a fantastic overcrowding, mitigated by such communal facilities as factory clubs, 'parks of culture and rest', and 'pioneer palaces' for children. In the older centres existing housing was used to the utmost, on the general principle of a family to each room or subdivided room. People moved into new housing well before the building was completed (this is still widespread, though at later stages of construction). Plans for new industrial centres included housing in the form of barracks and hostels, with the cost per family or per person kept as low as possible. This accommodation was administered by the factory management with the aid of the trade union, their function being to pack in as many people as possible. But it was far from enough, as the labour actually needed for the new industries was usually more than that planned; the consequence was a growth of 'shanty towns', consisting of makeshift dwellings put up by the incoming families themselves.

During the past 40 years the number of towns with over half a million population has increased from three to 30 and towns of

A street in Bukhara

100,000–500,000 inhabitants from 28 to 162. By the 1950s the view presented by such large and medium towns was, in many cases at least, a small central area containing the town soviet, party offices and other administrative buildings, a new theatre and cinemas, hospitals and various technical colleges and some streets of old or new blocks of flats, with more streets of small individual pre-1914 houses, mostly of timber; outside all this were large factories surrounded by hostels and club premises taking up the rest of the urban area, and pockets of shanty-town dwellings, extending in some cases for miles around the town, possibly including some old nearby villages occupied by the new townspeople.

It was not until the late 1950s that the feeble attempts by town soviets to get some order into these developments were reported in the newspapers. The effective authorities remained the factory managers backed by the town party bureaus. Except for the two principal cities of Moscow and Leningrad and some of the larger and politically important republic capitals, where the civic authorities were backed by the city party leaders or by the Politbureau itself, the soviets of the industrial towns were usually unable to prevent officials of the industrial ministries from marking out sites for new factories and their associated hostels which could not be provided with the minimum necessary services for the projected labour force. In general, the attitude of the town party authorities was: more industry, come what may. The USSR, which pioneered economic planning, was most backward in effective town planning. As in other spheres of public life, the Soviet government announced its intention of doing something about an evil by first allowing the facts to be reported. In 1957 a decree on housing admitted the urgency of the need, in general terms, and in 1960 a congress of town development was held in Moscow, at which some of the conditions were described and reported in the press. Since 1957 the soviets of the large and medium towns have been given more supervisory control over the factory housing and more planning and enforcement authority, both by legislation and by instructions from the central party authorities to the town party bureaus. Above all, there has been a very big increase in the allocation of materials and labour in the national plans to housing and associated services.

Destruction during the war, after which a large proportion of both industry and housing in European Russia had to be rebuilt, had aggravated the problem. When the Germans were being forced back from Russia it was decided not to rebuild in the haphazard way of the prewar five-year plans, but to plan the towns properly. In the event, the pressure from the same body which had taken this decision (the Politbureau) to rebuild and expand industry as fast as possible made nonsense of town planning. The earlier neglect of housing and amenities continued. It proved possible to rebuild and increase industry more quickly than had been expected. Towns in both the reconstructed areas

The communal kitchen

(Left) *washing facilities in a Moscow neighbourhood.* (Right) *a Moscow flat. A contrast in living standards*

and those which had not suffered invasion were soon in a worse condition than before the war, as the growth of urban population came vastly to exceed the anticipated figure. It is a tribute to the remarkable discipline of the Soviet press that, until the decision to put great resources into housing was taken in the late 1950s and journalists were permitted to write about it, the newspapers ignored this most acute problem of daily life.

Since 1958 about 70 million square metres of new housing has been built in the towns each year. During this period the urban population has risen by about $3\frac{1}{2}$ million people a year. This means that the new housing is equal to 170 square feet, or one medium-sized room, per additional person. The net increase in dwelling-space is less, since some old housing has been demolished to make way for the new. However, the overcrowding was so severe (for example, in Moscow, 40 square feet per head) that this rate of new construction has eased it despite the rise in town population. Far more important than the gain in space is the gain in privacy. For millions of families the nightmare of sharing with four, six or 10 other families the single kitchen and lavatory of a badly maintained pre-1914 flat has given way to the joy of a flat of their own. It is an emotional experience

to be shown by Russian friends around their new flat; the tiny size of
bathroom and kitchen, general gimcrack construction, thin walls
which may be no barrier to neighbours' noise, are almost irrelevant.
The new housing is mostly very small flats in very large blocks of
six to eight storeys, like huge boxes. This makes for a kind of over-
powering monotony in the new suburbs, relieved since the early
1960s by the use of colour and different lines of balconies, and more
recently by much taller blocks in some cities.

The ground floors are often used for shops, with the inner court-
yard serving as both the unloading space for vehicles and the children's
play area. In the cleared spaces and new suburbs of the great towns
these almost undifferentiated blocks stretch endlessly: again, the
principle is minimum cost and speed for the maximum number of
people, but with the fundamental difference of family privacy.
Until recently public opinion appeared to be in hearty agreement
with the government's policy of housing as many families as possible
in their own flats at the expense of variety and layout of blocks, size
of dwelling, standard of construction and provision of public buildings. One's own front door, kitchen and bathroom first; secondary
matters can wait. But, by mid-1968 public opinion had changed:
inhabitants of new flats were blaming Khrushchev for having ordered
quantity and speed regardless of quality, perhaps because all interior
repairs are paid for by the tenants. The standards of housing now
under construction are distinctly better.

Until about 1960 the flats in new state housing were let, and in

Nineteen-storey blocks of flats being built in Moscow

part designed, on the principle of one room per family, except for the privileged minority: thus the present policy of one flat per family irrespective of class is an important change in social policy. In the largest towns, factories are being kept out of the new housing areas. This construction of housing for its own sake, and not as an immediate appendage to industry, is another important departure in social policy. It means that a family is not evicted when a married man

'*The last in the queue need not wait – there isn't enough (of the complaints book) for everyone*'

changes or loses his job. Evictions are now possible only by court order. Almost every year since the crisis over Cuba in 1962 there have been rumours that housing construction was to be completely stopped, as if the town population, which is well aware of the strain on the government's resources and the sudden nature of policy reversals, could not trust its good fortune.

The new housing areas are now becoming the predominant element in the appearance of large and some medium-sized towns. In addition, the shanty areas on the outskirts of the newer industrial centres are giving way to small individual houses of much better construction, still put up by the continuing flow of newcomers, but with loans from the state for this purpose and—what is at least equally important— allocations of building materials obtained through a man's place of work or the town soviet, and technical assistance. These areas of individually owned and built houses are now more obvious in the smaller industrial and administrative centres, to which the big blocks of flats have not yet penetrated; roads, electricity, water supply and drainage are appearing amongst them. It is their inhabitants who own a large proportion of the 'town cows' on their allotments and live in semi-peasant style. For the great mass of young unmarried workers, and for millions of young couples still, industrial hostels are the main kind of dwelling. These can still be seen in plenty, especially in the

Prefabricated housing

newest towns and in the industrial construction sites which will become towns in due course. The hostels include many kinds of structure, from brick or prefabricated dormitory blocks, some of which are put up by the spare-time labour of their inhabitants under the auspices of their place of work, down to great permanent tents or Nissen-type sheds crammed with people.

Like the poorer type of hostel or barrack accommodation, the older housing in towns which existed before the revolution is regarded by the authorities as soon to be replaced and thus receives very little maintenance or repair. The author was astonished to find, on revisiting a street in Moscow where he had lived before the war, some small wooden houses which had been extremely dilapidated and not repaired at that time because of impending demolition, still there nearly 30 years later, inhabited and in even worse condition. Early this century half the housing in Moscow was this kind of building— very similar to the better kind of peasant wooden dwelling—and much of the present-day older provincial towns still consists of such houses, many of them still privately owned because they were too small and their owners too poor to be subject to nationalisation at the time of the revolution.

Privately owned housing in the towns amounts to a third of all the dwelling-space. It comprises the small individual dwellings, including the old ones just mentioned and the millions put up by immigrants from the countryside since the early 1930s. Some of the private housing consists of country cottages (*dachas*) to which the upper- and middle-class families in the big administrative towns retire in the hot summer months. Except for those owned by members of the wealthy or highly privileged class, the dachas are mostly primitive, depending on oil-lamps and a stream. Another category of privately owned dwelling, which has come into prominence during the past few years in connection with the campaigns against economic crime, are those, sometimes substantially built, which have been erected as an investment. The authorities have been confiscating without compensation houses whose owners cannot prove that they have earned the money and legally obtained the materials for their construction. (The writer visited in 1961 friends who had rented part of such a house in one of the Baltic republics: this building would have been worth about £8,000 in England. Its owner had built it, over many years, entirely with his own hands in his spare time, using materials whose origin was best known to himself. It was not quite completed and he had

New small houses in Volsk on the Volga River, built with state loans

just been informed of its confiscation.) Some town soviets have recently been confiscating 'second houses' belonging to families who have another house or are in a rented state flat. The second houses are the country dachas: there was dismay amongst the dacha community in Leningrad when the city boundaries were extended a few years ago and many such cottages became liable to confiscation. Collective farmers near resorts have built dachas on their household plots for renting or even sale at exorbitant prices to holiday-makers: the legal position, as in all matters relating to housing, is very tangled. A house is the main form of private property from which an income or even a small fortune can be made in the USSR. However, like the two other kinds of income-providing property (private cows, for sale of milk, and private cars used as illegal taxis), the difficulties, risks or insecurities are considerable. (For the sake of completeness, the only other private property which yields income should be noted here: money in the state savings bank, on which two or three per cent interest or lottery winnings are paid.)

Cooperative ownership and construction of housing has been encouraged and banned at different times. At present it is being strongly encouraged and is now responsible for about a tenth of the new housing in the towns. This is a middle-class activity. A typical case is a block containing 468 flats in Moscow, jointly owned by its inhabitants, all of whom have high salaries. They registered as a house-building cooperative, put up 40 per cent of the cost (the state lending the remainder for 15 years at three per cent interest), and with some difficulty obtained permission to engage a state construction agency and received allocation certificates for the necessary land and materials. This block is administered by a committee of the residents. Most of its flats are of two rooms, but there are some of three and even four. (The size of each flat, in relation to the family needs of its future occupant, had to be agreed beforehand with the housing authority.) Construction cost was about 4,000 rubles per two-roomed flat; monthly charges, including loan repayment, amount to 30 rubles. The law is not entirely clear as to whether residents own a theoretical proportion of the whole building or their actual flats: in effect, they are able to sell the actual flat on leaving, for construction cost less depreciation, without breaking the law. 'Key-money', however, can be very high—up to 30,000 rubles. Some towns now (mid-1968) have long queues of applicants for cooperative house-building. An official of lower middle rank, with plenty of money, applying on the grounds that his son, at fifteen, is too old to share the single room with his parents, was told to wait until the boy is old enough to earn his own living. A dentist, with a room 8 square metres (10 ×8½ feet) for his bed, possessions, equipment and private patients, is awaiting permission to join a cooperative housing scheme, after spending twelve fruitless years in the queue for a state flat.

State-owned housing, which now comprises most of the accommodation in the towns, includes three main types of building. There are the pre-1914 solidly constructed large dwellings—usually in flats of up to 10–12 rooms—confiscated from the wealthier classes at the time of the revolution, and since then inhabited by one or more family per original room, sometimes including descendants of the former owner and his family who were 'compacted' into one room. These buildings are now old and very poorly maintained. The main part of state housing is, by now, the new large blocks of flats described above, which are built, and mostly inhabited, on the principle of one family per flat. Some of these are erected and administered by state offices or academic institutions for their staff, but most are directly built, let and run by the town soviet. The third kind of state housing is the hostels and barracks which serve as the accommodation annexes of big industrial enterprises and for students. The common feature of all state housing is its low rent, which averages about five per cent of the tenant's pay or three per cent of total family earnings. It may vary with income and amount of amenities. As distinct from houses built individually by workers with the aid of a state loan, or cooperatively by the better-off professional people, the housing erected by state authorities, whether local soviets or factories, is regarded as a social service, and the construction cost, to say nothing of interest on it, is not recovered in the rent, which is calculated to cover only the cost of structural maintenance and administration. Thus rent is a relatively small item in the budget of most Soviet families. The true cost of modern housing is felt by those who can afford to join a housing cooperative, and the true market rent is paid by people who for one reason or another engage accommodation privately—in Moscow at around 50 rubles a room and 30 rubles for half a room per month.

Statistics on the quality of urban housing ceased to be published in the 1930s. A responsible American estimate is that in 1956, before the present house-building drive reached its full scope, nine-tenths of all Soviet urban housing had electric light, a third had running water, rather less had drainage, a fifth central heating, a seventh gas, one-twelfth a bath or shower and one-fiftieth hot water. The position

must have improved considerably since then. A 1967 Soviet publication gave the position in January 1963, 'for the centre, including
Moscow', i.e. the most developed area of the USSR, which has
received the lion's share of the new housing and services, as: space
per head, 6·4 square metres (70 square feet); piped water—60 per
cent of dwellings; drainage—59 per cent; central heating—56 per
cent; hot water—14 per cent; gas—49 per cent; bath or shower—39
per cent.

The 6·4 square metres per head just mentioned would be equivalent, for a family of three, to a room measuring 16 × 13 feet. The
'square metres' measure for housing is for living-rooms only; it does
not include the area of passages, pantries or bathrooms, or of communal kitchens in the shared flats. Everybody uses this measure.
Strangers chatting in a train may be telling each other how much they
earn and how many square metres they have—the two fundamentals
of Soviet urban life. People who wish to move from one part of
Moscow to another advertise in a special publication or stand outside
a certain cinema which is the unofficial housing market. Always, the
number of square metres is specified. Although bathroom space is
not included in housing area, the term 'free bathroom' in these
exchange negotiations means that nobody is actually living in the
bathroom. A Soviet professor visiting the home of a British university
lecturer insisted on measuring up all the rooms and came to the conclusion that he paid more rent per square metre in Moscow. Despite
the impression of tremendous housing construction in the USSR, it is
not very much greater than in Western countries. In 1965 the number
of units (flats or houses) built was as follows, per thousand population:
USSR—9·6; France—8·4; USA—7·9; Britain—7·3. The West German
figure now exceeds the Soviet, in proportion to population.

In addition to getting flats, people are now able to buy refrigerators,
washing machines, vacuum cleaners and television sets to put in
them. The quality of these goods is poor, as they are mostly made at
big engineering works, in whatever free space is available or in shops
built on to such factories. But the government is beginning to treat
their manufacture as industries in their own right and the scale of
production is increasing. Furniture and furnishings are sometimes
more difficult, because the demand occasioned by all the house-
building has not been matched by production. A Russian friend of
the writer had a roomful of books on the floor for years after moving
into a new flat: he had sworn to get decent bookshelves or none at all,
and the effort to get them, by purchase or the services of a joiner, had

taken much of his spare time. Middle-class Soviet citizens have started to become choosey, before it is wise to do so. Maintenance and repair facilities for domestic equipment are very inadequate. Specialist mechanics make quite high incomes in their spare time mending the shoddily manufactured electrical domestic goods. Skilled men on the new housing sites sometimes admit that they have a big stake in poor flooring, plumbing or wiring, as they are well paid privately for putting these right in their free time. It is said that good radio mechanics make most of all, not so much

A washing machine. (The stools are of a type much sought after)

in repairing sets (which are well made), as in modifying them to receive the Western broadcasts in Soviet languages. Urban transport is very cheap (three to five kopeks for any journey) but very inadequate, especially with people now living further from their work. Such services as laundries and hairdressing are still very poor. The citizens of Novosibirsk, the largest town in Siberia, spend on average nearly an hour every working day waiting for public transport, and in 1965 had only enough dry-cleaning facilities for one garment per person every seven or eight years. (The writer, having collected a suit from the cleaners in Leningrad just in time to wear it at a function, found that all the buttons had been cut off.) In the matter of reasonably good restaurants the shortage in many towns was desperate a few years ago and is still acute, now that an increasing number of people have the money and the desire to dine out; cheap eating-places are more numerous and factories are well provided with canteens. Hotels in the large towns are utterly inadequate to provide for both the increasing number of foreign visitors and the very large numbers of Soviet citizens on business journeys, to say nothing of citizens travelling for private purposes. Foreign visitors are not normally aware of the plight of Soviet travellers, who may be lucky to share a hotel room with half a dozen others.

Shopping facilities have been improving, but more slowly than housing. Soviet economists used to say that the small proportion of people working in retail distribution in their country (about two per cent of the employed population, compared with 12 per cent in the United States, for example) showed the greater efficiency of the Soviet economic system, but this claim is not now made, for it is realised that the time and energy spent by the Soviet public in shopping may amount to the greater waste. In human terms, the strain of shopping in Soviet conditions is very great. Although shops remain open late, there are nothing like enough of them. The sales method is extremely bureaucratic, to combat pilfering and embezzlement by sales people and shop managements: customers may have to stand in three queues for each section of a grocery shop; to choose the goods and have them cut, weighed, wrapped and invoiced; to pay; and to get the purchases in exchange for the receipt. Shops in the central areas of the big cities may appear spacious and well stocked, but in the back streets and the smaller towns the situation is visibly very different. To feed and clothe a family at a level acceptable to the bulk of the Western European working class, it is necessary in a Soviet city not only to have a high income but also for a servant to work full time shopping for food and finding out without delay when and where good-quality (which usually means foreign) clothing, footwear and domestic items are expected to appear, for these are likely to be sold out as soon as a shop gets any.

The years, from the late 1920s to the middle 1950s, when people thankfully bought whatever the shops had available, are over, but the time when it is possible to get what one wants has not yet arrived. In 1961 the writer, casually setting out to buy socks in Leningrad and rebelling at the shoddiness of what could be found, spent several hours exploring the shops of that great city in a determination to find at least one pair comparable to a cheap British kind, but was unsuccessful. This may sound trivial, and the accessibility and quality of clothing have moderately improved since then in Russia, but shopping is still an overwhelming triviality of daily life, especially for the great majority of women, who have to work and shop and look after a family. In 1964 people wishing to buy the better makes of refrigerator were put on a four-year waiting list. The days when the

An excellent shop at 'Academy Town', ten miles from Novosibirsk, whose inhabitants come there in preference to the city shops

planners of production and distribution could forget about sewing needles are probably over, but the public are not quite sure that this is so. Before the large imports of sugar from Cuba and recent increases in Soviet production, this commodity might turn up not more than two or three times a year in the shops of the smaller provincial towns. Flour is on sale, still, only on national holidays and election days. Visitors from even large provincial cities to Moscow or Leningrad are begged by acquaintances to bring back for them goods unobtainable at home. The towns of the USSR are divided into several priority categories in the national retail distribution plans, with Moscow uniquely favoured, Leningrad, Kiev and a few others next, and the small towns at the bottom—this is why men who drive long-distance lorries conduct an illegal but highly profitable side activity. (The villages have always been in a special category for supply, a long way below the smallest towns. In 1966, however, the surcharge on goods sold in villages was abolished and retail prices are now the same in country and town shops.) Soviet visitors to Western countries tend to be astonished not only at the number of shops and the range, quality and low prices of their contents, but at finding essentially the same wealth of foods, manufactured goods and services in towns of all sizes. They have in many cases heard about this, as they have about the amount and quality of ordinary housing, before their trip abroad, but the direct experience appears to be a strong one nevertheless.

A book could be written on the effect of planning upon Soviet consumer goods and services. Scheduled trains and aircraft are liable to be cancelled if seat bookings do not help to attain the high average percentage required by plan. The notorious heaviness of certain consumer durables has been due to the fact that the output plans were set, and their fulfilment measured, in weight. An informal investigation behind the scenes of a large restaurant convinced the writer that the planning system contributed a good deal to customers having to wait over an hour for a meal. Towards the end of a year, or quarter, public libraries may refuse to lend books in certain categories and will press upon borrowers books in other categories because the Ministry of Culture sets them plans of borrowings in each category—literature, popular science, technology, anti-religious works, etc.

COMMUNAL LIFE AND SOCIAL ORGANISATIONS

The relative privacy made possible by the new flats should not be confused with isolation. A large housing block or cluster of small blocks or a street of older housing teems with a variety of 'social organisations', such as a parents' committee connected with the local schools, a 'comradely court' for settling quarrels between tenants, a women's council, a commission for adolescents which provides guidance, a 'greenery group' which plants grass, flowers and trees, a repair detachment, an auxiliary militia detachment, groups for help to aged or sick tenants, a volunteer fire brigade, and a great variety of others. All these are voluntary bodies, the formation of which has been vigorously encouraged since the new party programme in 1961 declared that the USSR had entered the period of transition to Full Communism, with which the withering away of the state is vaguely associated. In practice, however, these bodies are most numerous in the blocks of new state housing, and their activities amount to an effort to preserve and develop the sense of community which, in other countries, is liable to be lost when people are moved out of old slums into new housing estates. Some of these organisations, in particular the comradely courts, have a long history, but most, however, are fairly recent creations. In the past few years almost all the new housing and much of the older type of flats have acquired house committees, which are similarly voluntary bodies whose function is to coordinate these activities, to encourage many more, and to act in the tenants' interests *vis-à-vis* the housing authority. A great variety of good works and self-help amongst the neighbours is undertaken by these committees.

Café in Sokolniki Park, Moscow

Russians tend to take it for granted that people are their brothers' keepers. Most of the new state housing has not much social differentiation between the lower middle and working classes: teachers, doctors, graduate engineers, minor officials, clerks, skilled and unskilled workers, are all neighbours together. There is a great sense of pride amongst some tenants in their new building, and a propensity not to care, and even to destroy, amongst others. In these circumstances it is natural for some to take the lead in preserving and developing the amenities, peace and good name of their dwelling.

The house committee is elected by the tenants as a whole. It has many sub-committees, including one for fabric and finance, which looks after maintenance and prompt payment of rent and the bills for central heating, electricity, gas, etc. The amenities sub-committee sets up and stimulates a greenery group and similar bodies. Such activities as establishing a 'Red corner' (small club facilities), a library, lectures and evening courses given by tenants in their own specialisations, are undertaken by the mass-cultural sub-committee. There is another section of the house committee which is concerned with the children of tenants; it helps the parents' council, adolescents' commission and similar bodies, including a variety of children's organisations, or gets them established in the block, and organises suitable tenants to run hobbies, sewing classes and games on the premises or to put young people in touch with appropriate outside institutions. In addition to keeping youngsters off the streets, this sub-committee is often active in arranging, through the connections of tenants, to help adolescents into suitable work and further education. The sanitary sub-committee is concerned in particular with bathrooms and kitchens: one report describes how in one block 250 badly kept flats were cleaned up by their occupants within a few days of a campaign being started. In a block of several hundred families several people—usually pensioners—may give much of their time and several dozen much of their free time on the house committee, its sub-committees and the various bodies mentioned, with a large proportion of the rest drawn occasionally into one or another of these activities. Nobody is paid for the work. The house committee gets part of a levy on rent of between one and two per cent for 'mass cultural work'. From this it equips the 'Red corner' (which may be one of the flats) with a television set, books, blackboard, etc., buys games and hobbies equipment for young people, establishes a children's playground for the summer and perhaps provides a washing machine for communal use. (Some domestic items such as vacuum cleaners and tools can be hired from state rental shops.) There is obviously scope for an expansion of such activities. Much of the work is in a negative direction at present, such as getting tenants not to foul their lavatories and to turn off taps when not in use.

The field of responsibility of a house committee is nothing less than the entire social and private life of the occupants. A movement has recently started for housing units to earn the title of 'House of Communist Daily Life', with cash prizes and banner-trophies for the best house committees, but whether there is anything more in this than the rather empty and enforced similar movements in industry, such as for the title 'Brigade of Communist Labour', it is not possible to say. The most exemplary family in a block gets a certificate to that effect. Some of the committees concentrate on slogans such as, 'Let there be no mutual abuse, slanders or quarrels between neighbours.' One block of flats is reported to have disbanded its comradely court because of the success of its house committee in introducing

View of Tashkent, old city, as reconstructed after the severe earthquakes of April–July 1966. The drawing gives an idealised impression. The positions of buildings in the middle and far distance have been altered to get them into the picture

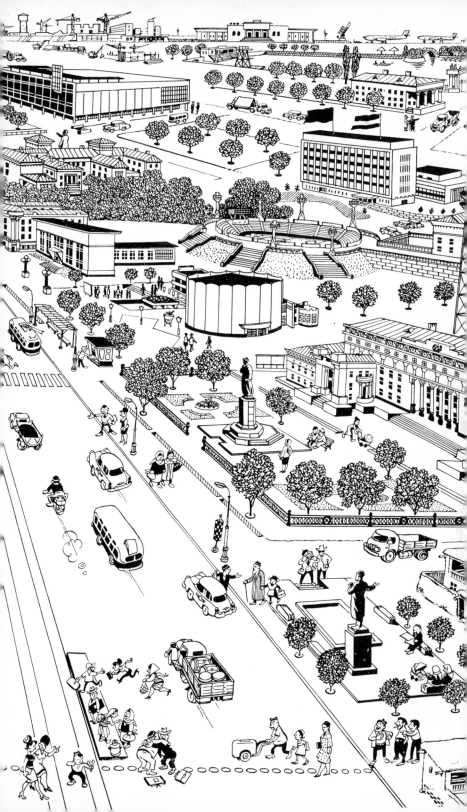

harmony. Some parents' committees organise regular meetings, widely attended by the adults, to which children report on their progress at school.

Since the house committees operate in large housing units of several hundred and sometimes several thousand families, there are 'stair' or 'entry' councils, elected by each group of families, under their auspices. These councils are in direct contact with the tenants and their main task is to prevent or report damage to the property, disturbances of the peace and bad living in general. Persistent offenders are interviewed at full meetings of the house committee or summoned to the comradely court, their misdeeds may be reported in the local newspaper or they may be recommended for eviction. In some places the auxiliary militia detachment based on a housing block has one or two members resident on every stairway who can summon their comrades when necessary or call in the regular militia.

There is less scope for self-administration in the industrial and student hostels, where each floor or section elects a committee which allocates duties for tidying up. Such administration as is practised by the inhabitants tends to be concentrated in the hands of the Young Communist League branch at the factory or educational institution. The house committees in local authority housing are not directly controlled by the Communist Party, because political organisation is based on the place of work, not habitation. This fact could allow unusual scope for spontaneous development of the house committees, now that an increasing proportion of the population is living in housing which is not associated with any one place of work. But in practice the house committees are subservient to the party organisations in the local departments of the housing authorities, and the most active leaders of the house committees are often retired party officials. The old street committees remain, both in areas of the older type of flats and where the private individual houses are predominant, but they have little significance in the former and virtually none in the latter. By a curious law of 1956, which resuscitated an old Russian tradition, the street committees, and similarly the house committees when they came into being in 1959, were empowered to convene mass meetings of inhabitants which could order by simple vote the exiling of any neighbour considered to be an 'idler' or 'parasite'. This power was modified in 1965.

Amongst the voluntary bodies in the big new blocks and the hostels, civil defence groups should be mentioned. These are active in drill, study and the preparation of makeshift shelters against atomic and gas attack. They are voluntary in a limited sense, as are the local groups—many of which are based on housing units—of the Voluntary Association for Collaboration with the Army, Aviation and Fleet. A third association closely related to these two, with branches in the big housing units, is the Red Cross and Red Crescent Society.

The most important, numerically, of the voluntary bodies mentioned is the auxiliary militia, which were first established on a large scale by a government and party decree in 1959 to combat 'hooliganism' which was becoming serious. By 1964 they had six million members, mostly young men, who wear armbands and patrol potential trouble spots in small groups, with powers of arrest in emergency. In some towns they are given shop windows in which they put the names, addresses, photographs and details of local people whom they consider objectionable. Some small towns have been physically terrorised by these organisations and the regular militia have often been doubtful about their value. They may, however, do much good in many places: poor street lighting, drunkenness and violence are frequent enough in Soviet towns. In practice, the auxiliary militia have been controlled by the town party leaders and the KGB rather than by the regular militia. Their importance is now (1968) declining. There is also a children's version of the auxiliary militia based on housing units. The oldest amongst the many kinds of social organisation now existing are the comradely courts, which consist usually of three or five judges elected at a dwelling or place of work to settle disputes on the spot or to bring the social disapproval of neighbours or workmates to bear on an offender. These courts may impose small fines, but their power lies primarily in the personal authority of the judges and the attitude of those present, which can be very effective; they also have a traditional right to ask the local public prosecutor to bring a criminal charge in the official court against an offender.

There are many more such overlapping social organisations now in existence. The extent to which they are linked to official bodies, or with their counterparts in other housing units or factories, varies greatly, as does the directing influence over them exercised by the party or Young Communist League, which in most cases depends on local circumstances and personalities. The house committees are still in a very formative stage; their links and relations with the housing commission of the town soviet and the central and local staffs of its housing department are somewhat different in every town. There is

already a body of central government legislation on the house committees which gives them the right, amongst others, to inspect the
books of the local housing authority. However, none of the writer's
acquaintances in several Russian and Ukrainian towns, asked about
these committees in mid-1968, regarded them as much more than a
powerless link between the housing offices and the tenants.

As has been indicated above, the principle behind these communal
organisations may owe as much to traditional patterns of Russian
behaviour as to Communist theory. Anybody who has lived in Russia
must have encountered instances of groups—even accidental groups
of people who do not know each other—acting as units and having
a unanimous group opinion, or being assumed to so act or think. A
few years ago the writer was the only passenger in a bus when the
driver pulled up, jumped down and bought a melon, although there
was a long queue at the shop. The writer then followed the driver's
example, but was told to wait in the queue, at which the driver
protested. The writer apologised and retreated, but the driver insisted
that he be served and the saleswoman refused. The driver then asked
the queue and one or two people in it appeared to consent. He
immediately shouted, 'The queue has decided', and the writer bought
a melon.

TOWN SOVIETS

Such power as a town soviet exercises resides in its executive committee, the core of which consists of people on the nomenklatura
list of the town party bureau. The executive committee is, in effect,
the arm of the bureau for purposes of local government. In thousands
of cases the chairman of the executive committee is not even a member
of the soviet because the bureau has not thought it worth while to
arrange the requisite by-election on putting a new man in this post.
The ordinary deputies to the town soviet are also selected by the
town party authorities, on the universal principle of one candidate
per constituency. In effect, the mass of deputies (one per 350 electors
in the small and medium towns) constitutes the liaison between the
population and the executive committee of the soviet. There is a
high turnover of deputies at the two-yearly elections, enabling many
of the more solid citizens to acquire some experience of this office.
Their liaison function is performed mainly in the standing commissions of the soviet, which are numerous—for health, education,
trade, pensions, housing, culture, militia, eating-places, adolescents,
greenery, fire services and so on. Each standing commission has a

few deputies, usually under a member of the executive committee, and a larger number of citizens who sit on it by invitation or are informally elected to it by colleagues at their place of work or by neighbours, to whom they report back. These citizens include many of the more active people in the voluntary social organisations, and may be encountered in schools, hospitals, shops, pension and housing administrations and many other institutions, inspecting what goes on and asking the sometimes embarrassed staff what can be done to facilitate their work. It is not always clear whether they are doing this in their capacity as members of a standing commission of the soviet or as 'activists' in a voluntary organisation. For good measure, more millions of citizens are brought into civic activity at every election, as members and helpers of the electoral commissions, which check the voting lists and supervise the polling places: there were nine million members of electoral commissions in the local elections of 1967.

Thus there is a continuous chain of civic activity, from the passive citizen who likes to hear the neighbours' children report their examination results, or the office worker persuaded to help at an election, up through the house committees and standing commissions to membership of the town soviet. Another chain, that of political power, links on to it inside the executive committee of the soviet, passes through the town party bureau, and thence up the hierarchy of party bodies. A weaker chain, of the state's administrative authority, goes up from the town soviet, through province and republic soviets, to the Supreme Soviet of the USSR.

An American student of Soviet local government was recently given the unusual opportunity of seeing one of the ward soviets of Moscow in operation. A meeting of its executive committee dealt in a fairly businesslike way with questions which mostly concerned the modernisation of housing in a part of Central Moscow. (The character of the area was to be preserved by installing bathrooms, etc., instead of demolishing and rebuilding: the problem was to keep up to plan on this work, which was being delayed by the fact that the occupants had nowhere else to go.) A meeting of the full soviet, held in a theatre, was by comparison almost farcical. The proceedings consisted of a long, monotonous and selective report given by the chairman on behalf of the executive committee and dutifully accepted by the soviet after a few desultory speeches and questions. The several hundred members of the soviet appeared to be more interested in the fruits, not available in shops, which were on

A fashion show, Moscow

sale to them in the foyer. The American also spent half a day in the office of the assistant chairman when he received visitors with personal housing problems. He decided most of the applications on the spot, quickly, sensibly and not bureaucratically, in the light of the laws and by-laws. The American, who was emotionally drained by this experience, conceived an admiration for the competence and toughness of this official, who told him that his previous job—as assistant manager of a factory—had been more exacting.

THE STANDARD OF LIVING

Almost everybody working in the towns is state-employed. There are two kinds of exceptions, legal and illegal. The legal exceptions comprise, in the main: domestic servants, usually village girls who manage to get a passport and a place to live by this means as a step towards study or work in a town; self-employed craftsmen, who are heavily taxed and otherwise discouraged by the authorities; and members of the 'free professions' such as authors, painters, composers and advocates who sell their work, but have to be in their official association, which is in some respects like a state-employing organisation. The illegal exceptions are town-dwellers not 'written in' by the militia, who live, often with relatives or paying very high rents, in semi-hiding and make a living somehow, but cannot get a legally recognised job without the militia's permission to be in the town. However, all those not in state employment amount to very few per cent of the occupied town population.

The official figure for average pay in state employment was 103

rubles a month in 1967. In the towns it is a little higher, because
wages in state jobs in the countryside, which include state-farm
workers, are relatively low. Thus average pay in the towns is worth
about £50 at the official exchange rate of 9s. 3d. to the ruble after the
British devaluation of November 1967. The actual purchasing
power of the ruble varies very much, according to patterns of
family expenditure and locality. Between four and five rubles to the
pound is the writer's estimate (see Appendix, p. 187). This would
make average pay nearer £25 a month. But average pay covers a
range from the legal minimum of 60 rubles up to salaries of 1,000 and
even 2,000 rubles (excluding higher earnings by the most widely
published writers, etc., who probably do not exceed a few hundred
in number and can be ignored here). There have always been, for
various reasons, many state-employed people getting less than the
legal minimum wage, and it would be realistic to put the extremes of
full-time pay for state-employed adults in the towns at 30 to 2,000
rubles. These extremes do not involve very large numbers of people,
however, in relation to the 80 million state-employed persons.
Unfortunately, no information is issued on urban income distribution.
It is certain that the great majority of townspeople in state employment, probably over 90 per cent, are paid between 60 and 150 rubles
a month. At the value of the ruble assumed above, Soviet pay in
rubles per month is equivalent to British purchasing power in shillings
per week. Thus the range of 60–150 rubles would be equivalent
to a range of £3 to £7 10s. a week in Britain.

This does not take into account, for the lower paid, the value of
thefts from the place of work (especially shops, dining-rooms,
warehouses and factories) and odd jobs; working at more than one
job, embezzlement and bribe-taking in the middle-income groups of
professional people, small executives and officials; and perquisites
in the higher groups. The size of these supplementary sources of
effective income is impossible to estimate. They are all important,
but perquisites are by far the most important in their effect on
standards of living. An example from a provincial capital is the
Second Secretary of the province party, who summoned an acquaint-
ance of the writer, the director of a state farm, for an afternoon's
work. The director himself enjoyed perquisites worth several times
his salary, but was impressed by the Second Secretary's access to
wealth when the latter telephoned for a case of the best beer and
50–60 eggs to be brought in. The two men disposed of these pro-
visions, putting a raw egg into each glass of beer and swallowing it

with the last gulp, thus preserving clear heads, though the director
could not eat for a few days afterwards. (The more or less secret
system of 'packets', whereby holders of medium and high posts of
political responsibility received cash on each pay-day amounting to
several times their regular salary, but not included in the ordinary
accounts or for income tax, was abolished in the late 1950s.)

THE WORKING CLASS

There is no systematic statistical information on Soviet working-class
incomes and expenditures, or indeed on any other aspect of this class.
It is not unfair to say that there are far less data for the working class
in the USSR than for any other industrial country in the world.
However, local surveys made for special purposes are beginning to
appear. One such, made in the big Urals factory town of Sverdlovsk,
to demonstrate the equalising effect of social services on family
incomes, was published in December 1967. It throws a little light
on the range of incomes within the working class, in relation to size
of families. The survey covered 888 families of workers in four
factories. It does not appear to have included the lowest-paid, or
anybody above the rank of foreman (it might, however, include
young married graduate technicians without children). The range
of family income groups reported is 59–214 rubles per month. The
lower-paid had much larger families than the higher-paid and fewer
earners per family, the range of income per family member being
14 and 97 rubles. This difference between the extreme groups in the
survey is greatly reduced by the social services, which are evaluated
at 94 rubles per family for the lowest and 17 rubles for the highest
income groups, making a total family income of 153 and 231 rubles
respectively. The social services evidently include health and
education, sickness benefits, pensions and children's allowances,
but they are not defined in the report and may include rent rebates
and non-statutory relief: they drop very sharply from the poorest to
the second poorest group. However, social services in Britain are at
least as good in relation to wages, so may be omitted in a comparison.

   The family income range of 59–214 rubles per month would be
worth, assuming that the pattern of expenditure by both types of
family makes their ruble worth between 4s. and 5s., about £3 and
nearly £11 per week respectively. The principles on which the
investigated families were selected are not stated. There are six
families in the poorest group and 57 in the best-off. The great

majority of the families in the survey (673 out of the 888) are classified in groups with family earnings ranging from 113 to 188 rubles per month, or from nearly £6 to £9 10s. per week. The number of earners per family in these groups is 1·5 and 1·9 respectively, which means that the average wage in each group is 75 rubles and 99 rubles, worth about £3 15s. and £5 per week respectively. However, the second earner, usually the wife, would normally earn less than her husband because, although women get equal pay for equal work, they are mostly in lower-paid occupations. Thus, if only the man were working, the respective family earnings would be nearer £4 and £6 per week. It is clear that the wife's earnings make a vital difference at this low standard of living, which is characteristic of the great mass of the working class in the USSR.

A survey of wages and prices in Moscow, London, Paris, Munich and New York, made in 1964 by a British economist familiar with these cities, comes to the following conclusions on the cost of the same 'basket' of food, designed to feed a family of four for a week: Moscow—32·78 rubles; London—£6 8s. 5d.; Paris—96·36 francs; Munich—83·98 DM; New York—$18·43. The earnings per hour of adult male industrial workers are then compared, to ascertain the working time necessary to buy this 'basket', with the following result: Moscow—65 hours; London—18¼ hours; Paris—21½ hours; Munich—20¾ hours; New York—8 hours. The limitations of any such comparison are, of course, considerable, especially in view of differences in the kinds of food available and bought, but these figures can be taken as some indication of the position.

The economist mentions his personal estimate of quality, range of choice and convenience of shopping, taking New York as 100: Moscow—30; London—75; Paris—70; Munich—55, but these subjective factors are not included in the results on costs and working time. The food element in the Soviet standard of living is on the same level as in the USA, Britain, France and Germany in one basic respect, namely a consumption of about 3,000 calories per person per day. However, the starch content in the Soviet diet is very high: a Russian working-class family eats about three times as much bread, for example, as its American counterpart. If we add the two other main constituents of working-class family consumption, namely housing and clothing, the Soviet family would probably come out worse still. Although rent is very low the amount and quality of accommodation are also low, while the cost of clothing is relatively very high and its quality is mostly very low. It is, in fact, difficult for a foreigner to ascertain how working-class families manage to clothe themselves, until he realises how much is earned in spare-time, quasi-legal and illegal activities. Schoolchildren have to wear school uniforms, which are of relatively good cloth and expensive; these are handed on for several generations of wearers until they cannot be further mended. (The state makes an immense profit on clothing: in mid-1968 the writer was given instances of around 700 per cent. For example, the cost of production of a garment selling at over eight rubles is 1·01 rubles. The profit made on children's clothes and footwear is, however, lower.)

Official figures have been published for consumption of the main foods, averaged over the entire population of the USSR, per person in the year 1965. If we take the latest prices in the state food shops, the cost would come to 350 rubles per person for the year, or just under a ruble a day. The average *spent* on food, however, must have been less because in the countryside and many of the smaller towns most or much of the meat, milk, eggs, potatoes and vegetables consumed is grown by the family itself. This is included in the average consumption. There is no information as to whether the amounts consumed are lower or higher for the urban than the rural population, or the position of those townspeople who live a semi-rural life (they own several million pigs and cows). Nor is there any statistical information about differences in food consumption between the different social and geographical sections of the fully urban population—say, the 80 millions who live in towns of over 50,000 inhabitants. Thus the average figures of food eaten tell us little about the diet of the main mass of the working class, which is known by observation to be strikingly inferior to that of the middle and upper classes and different in composition to that of the rural and semi-rural population.

An English housewife with some dietetic knowledge, asked to suggest a balanced, adequate and economical food budget at Soviet prices, proposed the following average quantities per person per day for a couple with two children of middle school age, assuming that a housewife's time is available for the necessary shopping and cooking. The items would consist of one pint of milk (in the form of buttermilk or sour cream: fresh milk is not normally used), one egg or one ounce of cheese, $\frac{1}{2}$ lb. of vegetables (cabbage and beetroots, which are popular in Russian soups, carrots and onions), $\frac{1}{2}$ lb. of bread (allowing some white as well as rye) and buckwheat porridge or potatoes, one ounce butter or margarine, one ounce sugar or jam, $\frac{1}{4}$ lb. of meat or fish, some tea, salt, flavourings and herbs. The cost—about 1·35 rubles a day at the lowest Moscow prices in 1968—would be reduced by substituting pulses for part of the meat or fish. Shopping in the collective farm markets would increase the cost, but the food would be fresher and better than in the state shops. For example, potatoes in the state shops are usually spoilt by frost, which makes perhaps half of the weight unusable. However, even the minimum theoretical cost of just under 40 rubles per head per month is too high for working-class incomes. A Soviet sample survey in 1963 indicated that families with incomes of up to 50 rubles

ИДУ ВСТРЕЧАТ

1. Цельнокроеное платье из гипюра, дублиров. на чехле. У горловины толочки его присобраны. длинный, с манжетом. И воротник-стойка, и манжеты цены брошами, гармонирующими с цветом платья. застежка-«молния». Размер 44—48.

2. Нарядное платье из тонкой шерстяной ткани ширенное от проймы. Воротник и планка из наряджев, контрастирующих с цветом платья.

3. Платье-костюм из ткани «космос». Жакет уме и несколько расширен от проймы, рукава. Наряд ум застежкой и бантом из шифонов блестящей ткани. немного расширена книзу. Размер 44—46.

4. Нарядное цельнокроеное платье из кружево лотна, дублированного шелковым атласом. Глубоки

Рисунки С. ДЕМЕНТЬЕВОЙ

20

Late 1967: fashionable dresses with short skirts

per head spent nearly 60 per cent of their outlays on food. A group of Soviet economists and sociologists have calculated, but not published, the income necessary for a decent minimum standard of living for Soviet urban families as 81·40 rubles per person (children and adults) per month at 1965 prices. They include, for example, one suit for a man each two years plus a pair of trousers each $1\frac{1}{2}$ years and a pair of shoes per year (far from excessive in view of the quality of clothing and footwear); a weekly cinema visit and a visit to the theatre once in two months. Very few of the families in the Sverdlovsk survey had an income per head as high as this.

THE MIDDLE AND UPPER CLASSES

Western sociologists are beginning to try to analyse the structure of Soviet society. So far, they have got nowhere. The main reason is lack of data. Another reason is that new concepts have to be thought up because social stratification in the USSR does not follow Western lines, but no satisfactory new concepts have yet been suggested. In this section, therefore, we have to fall back on the familiar terms 'middle class' and 'upper class' for those families in the towns who are in income, or in prestige, authority, education, privilege or other ways above the manual working class. After the revolution there was an important sense in which the working class had the highest prestige—in the minds of people who accepted Marxism—but this special prestige petered out before the war and does not exist now. The self-denying ordinance by which the income of party members was not to exceed that of a skilled worker lasted a much shorter time.

The Soviet middle class does not, so far as income is concerned, include the great majority of educated people in the 'mass professions', such as doctors, secondary school and technical college teachers and graduate engineers and technicians, as these get mostly up to 120–130 rubles a month, with limited opportunities for additional earnings. They are thus at the income level of the upper working class, and not very much above it even if both husband and wife are in the mass professions, but their higher education, social outlook, tastes and professional responsibilities distinguish them sharply from the working class. They form a large, rapidly growing and important element in the population and life of the big and medium towns. We shall call them the lower middle class, although this term has a rather different connotation in Western countries.

The pay zone of about 150–300 rubles may contain around five per cent of the urban working population. It includes people from the mass professions who have reached special positions of authority, such as factory engineers promoted to junior managerial level, medical men in charge of polyclinics or small hospitals and the junior and middle teaching staffs of universities. Many of the older people at this level of pay, such as responsible civil servants or experienced journalists, do not have higher education, but it is now extremely difficult for people without higher education to make such careers and get into this salary group. The possibilities of additional earnings, legal or illegal, improve considerably in this group, which may be regarded as the Soviet 'middle middle' class. Actual earnings tend to bunch around or above 300 rubles, leaving something of a gap in the income zone of, say, 150–250 rubles.

It is likely that not more than one or at most two per cent of the

*Office workers returning home: 6 o'clock in the Nevsky Prospect,
Leningrad*

urban working population are paid more than 300 rubles a month. These people usually have ample opportunities for extra earnings and special bonuses and—for those in positions of substantial business or party authority—many material perquisites and other privileges. This may be called the upper middle class. It still includes many elderly people who were promoted in the later 1930s after a rather rough-and-ready training, but for younger members a higher education is now more or less essential. Pay and additional legitimate earnings in this class stretch up to around 1,000 rubles. A full professor's salary is 450 rubles and he usually earns more in fees; a colonel gets 400 rubles, with more privileges. The manager of a medium-sized factory will make, with normal bonuses, 500–700 rubles, and more if engaged on military production; his senior staff will earn not very much less, but he has more perquisites and privileges. Other criteria may be far more important than salary in this class. There are great differences, for example, between people getting 300–350 rubles a month. An assistant head of department in an industrial ministry, who may be second in charge of the production of all automobile engines or footwear, gets 350 rubles. He has very great bureaucratic power, but no political power and not much prestige. The First Secretary of a province party bureau is also paid about 350 rubles but his perquisities, power, status and privileges put him in the upper class. The other secretaries (there are usually five, each responsible for one aspect of the life of the province) are paid around or below 300 rubles, but on the other criteria they stand high in the upper middle class and have good prospects of joining the upper class. The editor-in-chief of a popular magazine gets about 300 rubles and has good scope for earning more: he has considerable political responsibility but no power, and his position in the upper middle class is not high. (There are some industrial workers, such as drivers of large excavators, who regularly earn 300–350 rubles: they express their sense of status by refusing the small change in their pay.)

Although people at the higher income levels of this group can spend fairly freely, they live below the material standard of their Western counterparts, mainly because good housing, clothing and gadgets are so difficult to come by. They like to spend their money on good food and foreign clothes, on high fees for private treatment by the most competent doctors and dentists and on private tuition for their children. Social attitudes in this class and the upper class tend to be exclusive amongst the older people, who are themselves of worker or peasant origin. The architect mentioned on pp. 156–7 threatened to disown his son if he married a fellow-student, because she came from a collective farm.

As for the Soviet upper class, its members may be regarded primarily as the people who exercise political power—the party hierarchy down to the political leaders of provinces and important towns. The increasing number of people who come and go between these political levels and

New sanatorium in Sochi

the highest levels of state administration should be included. In Stalin's time members of the Politbureau did not need money, although they received salaries, because their living expenditures were made a charge upon the state, without effective limit. This selective instalment of Full Communism is mentioned here as the logical outcome of the access to wealth enjoyed by the political upper class. Amongst the younger members of this class, and at levels higher than province Second Secretaries, tastes may be more sophisticated than beer with raw eggs. The decision-making powers of this class in economic matters were noted in an earlier chapter. If we add its access to consumer goods and services, the grounds for considering this class as, in effect, the owner of the Soviet economy are strengthened.

The top professionals, such as the senior generals, full members of the central Academy of Sciences, directors of key factories and the most successful authors have effective incomes and privileges which bring them almost into the same material standards as the political personalities enjoy, and may in this limited respect be placed in the upper class. There is an elaborate system of 'closed' shops, hotels and other facilities, restricted to various groups of this class, where the highest quality is available at very reasonable (sometimes nominal) prices and excellent service is provided. These are the Soviet equivalent of the most exclusive shops and services in the Western countries, where access is restricted by price, but the difference in the West between the most exclusive and the ordinary is small in comparison with the Soviet situation. The 'closed shop' system extends down, in modified form, to privileged groups of the upper middle class—and to anybody with hard foreign currency. (The specialised hard-currency shops for food, clothing, footwear, gadgets, etc., where Western quality and range are available at Western prices, are also being made accessible to certain categories of middle-class Soviet citizens—for example, those who work with foreigners and need good clothes—to whom certificates for specific purchases are issued. In the large towns people know about these fabulous shops, but cannot even get in to look without hard currency or certificates. The process of issuing certificates is called certification. A bitter joke circulating in 1968 misquotes Lenin's famous definition of Full Communism as 'Soviet power plus the electrification of the entire country', replacing 'electrification' by 'certification'.)

There is a similar range of quality in the hospitals and clinics of the health service, and in shops selling medical supplies, from superb standards for the upper class to a distinctly poor service for the general public. As for housing, Stalin used to award good flats to people as a mark of personal esteem: on a less individualist basis, the practice is still normal in relations between the state and members of the more privileged groups. 'Personal pensions' on a generous scale are granted to the immediate relatives of deceased members of the upper class. Personal property is freely heritable, with no inheritance tax.

Income tax has little effect on wealth, as the maximum rate is 13 per cent. The system is simple and is remarkably near to a flat rate on all incomes from the legal minimum upwards. Tax starts at 60 rubles; on the income range 70–100 rubles it is 4·60 rubles plus 12 per cent on the amount of income over 70 rubles; on the range 100 rubles to infinity it is 8·20 rubles plus 13 per cent on the amount of income over 100 rubles. The sole allowance is a 30 per cent reduction if there are at least three dependants living with the assessed person. An able-bodied wife under 55 is not a dependant. Freelance earnings are assessed at an additional 10 per cent approximately. There is also a tax of six per cent on bachelors and on married people with no children, irrespective of income. There is virtually no direct local taxation. Ten years ago the government promised to abolish income tax, but has not yet done so, although its

A 'closed' bar. Like certain shops this bar accepts only foreign currency

importance in the budget revenue is small compared with turnover tax (purchase tax) and profits of state industry. A small step towards abolition—or towards the principle of progressive taxation—was made in 1968, when the Ministry of Finance was instructed to reduce the rate, as given above, by about 25 per cent for incomes below 80 rubles.

Apart from help to relatives and friends, the upper middle and upper classes have neither the habit nor any channels of benevolent or charitable use of money. A professor of literature with a salary of 450 rubles a month puts his spare money in the savings bank on deposit account at three per cent interest. The idea of giving any to a good cause has not occurred to him, as there are no good causes for private donations. This man pays about 50 rubles a month in dues to various organisations: 2·50 rubles to the Union of Soviet Writers and 10 rubles to the union's benevolent fund; five rubles to the Union of Soviet Journalists; one per cent of his salary to his trade union; and three per cent of his total income to the Communist Party. These are not donations but dues required of him as a member of these bodies. His contribution to good causes is in the form of time, and in this he is typical of his kind. He gives a third of his active time to unpaid service for 'social organisations', most of it as rector of an adult educational institution, called a 'People's University'. Since he makes in addition to his salary 400–500 rubles a month (an unusually high amount for a man of his status) from ideologically correct books and articles on literature, which are easily written and also take up a third of his time, he is foregoing this amount of money by his unpaid social work. But, with relatively little access to 'closed' shops, he finds it very difficult to spend his net income of about 700 rubles. He staunchly upholds the principles and policies of his party, but cannot help being overwhelmed by the shopping centre of a Western city.

Not only is private charity abnormal; it is illegal, insofar as any degree of officially unauthorised organisation is involved in the collection and distribution of money. Members of that section of the Baptist Church which opposes the officially recognised Baptist leaders, and which is essentially a working-class and peasant movement, have been imprisoned for organising financial help from amongst themselves for their needy brethren.

SECURITY AND EXPECTATIONS

Soviet families give very little thought to saving. Prolonged unemployment is not regarded as a serious possibility, while sickness benefit and retirement pensions are very good in relation to the wage level. Pensions begin at 60 for men and 55 for women (and earlier for underground and certain other jobs, for working mothers of large families, blind persons and dwarfs). The pension range is 30–120 rubles, depending on earnings: for most townspeople, who earn between 60 and 100 rubles, it is 45–52 rubles a month. But for men who have been in employment less than 25 years and women less than 20 years the pension is reduced proportionately. Benefits for industrial illness or injury are the same as earnings. Other sickness benefit depends on membership of a trade union and period of employment: for most townspeople, who have worked for at least eight years continuously and are trade union members, it is the same as earnings. There are no widows' pensions as such, but some small provision is made for dependants on the death of the breadwinner; this, however, is limited to dependants incapable of work for age or other reasons.

There are no contributions from wages for pensions or sickness pay, or for the health service, which is free (except for medicines and some state clinics), as is also education at all levels.

Another reason for the indifferent attitude to saving is that wages are too low. The only large section below the upper middle class that can afford to save consists of those working-class young men and women who are earning better than the average and living cheaply in the industrial hostels, but they tend to stock up on clothes rather than put money by for marriage. Even in middle-class families there is no substantial parallel to the life-insurance policies and other savings habits of Western countries, though its beginnings may be seen in the form of cooperative housing. When the government announced its agreement with the Fiat company, people began to put money by in anticipation of free sale of cars. Whatever the reasons for indifference to saving, the sense of security of employment is a psychological factor of fundamental importance in the Soviet standard of living for all social classes.

Other psychological factors may be noted, though they cannot be evaluated. Differences in the standard of living, both within the working class and between the classes, are now appreciably smaller than they were in Stalin's time. But the lines between the classes and sub-classes are now more difficult to cross. In that period the possibility of advance, whether for individuals or for the country as a whole, was more prominent in people's minds than it is now, even though the established town population was at that time glad to get by at all. Now there is a strong feeling in both the working and the middle classes that they could and ought to live much better than they do in many respects. The three great avenues of improvement before the war were: for the peasants, movement to the construction sites and towns; for the younger townspeople, the new opportunities of education and industrial skills; and the general sense, however vague or ironical, that the five-year plans were making Russia able to defend itself and provide a good life, if only for their children. Whatever else was experienced at that time, and whatever one may think on the question of whether Stalin was really necessary, the plans did embody for people their own deliberate transformation of a meagre inheritance. This special satisfaction of transforming the country does not now exist. Material advance is evident now, in housing, the 60-ruble minimum wage, the five-day week and in many other respects. But it does not amount to much. Everybody knows that the strong foundation has been established and that its

fruits in material things, time really for oneself and freedom from
hypocrisy, bullying and fear could be much greater. But nobody
knows what to do about it and no serious public discussion of how to
get the country out of this uneasy stupor is allowed. The government
expects everybody to applaud its half-hearted attempts to hide the
enormous problem under an ideological rag of Full Communism,
while the year 1980 has become officially unmentionable, although
it remains the key point in the party's programme, and even the
jokes made about it in Khrushchev's time are forgotten.

THE CITIES AND THE INDUSTRIAL FRONTIER

Nearly half the inhabitants of the towns are immigrants who were
born on the land. Nowadays people want to move from the smaller or
more remote towns to the biggest cities of European Russia, Moscow
especially. People are not allowed to settle in them without very
special reasons, but these restrictions are evaded. Amongst the
older small and medium towns, many have either insufficient or
unattractive prospects of employment and education; industrialisation
has passed them by or made them dependent upon a single industry
(as in Shuya, population 69,000, the textile town of single women
where the planners are only now beginning to provide jobs for men).
The more energetic young people get out of these backwaters. The
planners are now finding difficulty in developing the industrial
centres of Siberia, as more people are leaving them for the European
area than can be induced to emigrate to them. It is no longer practicable, as it was in the 1950s, to use the Young Communist League as
a mobiliser of young workers for areas in need of development,
while the planners have not yet learned how to cope with human
preferences which run counter to government policies.

The European centres are becoming more alike, with the same
big housing blocks, underground railways and traffic jams. Moscow
(population 6½ million) has the bright lights (in neon advertisements
of Lenin and Communism) and the fullest shops. To have a passport
issued in Moscow (i.e. the right to live there) is to be especially
fortunate. But the capital has something oppressive as the hub of an
authoritarian system and the centre of an over-administered faith
which has lost its vitality. The cultural opportunities are fairly rich
and very much used; at the same time everybody seems to be
concentrating on earning a few more rubles. Leningrad (3,665,000)
is not basically different, although to the foreign outsider it seems so

—perhaps because of a less heavy sense of secular and ideological authority, its civic pride, the classical dignity of its central architecture and touches of the same element in its manners. Volgograd (Stalingrad, 720,000), officially one of the 'hero-cities',

Moscow Underground

stretches interminably along the bank of the great river. Minsk (750,000), the capital of the Byelorussian republic, is more lively and colourful than Russian towns of its size. The Ukrainian cities also have more character: Kiev the capital (1,383,000), with its long tradition as the first centre of the Russian state and religion, and the natural beauty of its setting; Odessa (753,000) on the Black Sea, which has not entirely lost its pre-revolutionary commercial reputation and where nearly all things foreign, including literature, can be obtained; and Kharkov (1,092,000), the dour administrative centre of Ukrainian heavy industry which is equivalent in size to that of Britain. Riga (669,000), Tallinn (335,000) and to a lesser extent Vilnius (309,000), the capitals of the Baltic republics, remain Western cities on which Soviet overcrowding has descended since the war.

In Asia, the Transcaucasian capitals retain their distinct characters. Tbilisi (830,000), obstinately Georgian in language and way of life, surprises Russian visitors as being somehow un-Soviet in the easy-going appearance of its street life. Baku (1,175,000), in Moslem Azerbaijan, is a polyglot centre of the oil and engineering industries. Erevan (652,000) is a capital for Armenians all over the USSR and the world, not only of the relatively small number living in the republic. The Central Asian capitals, in their oases or mountains, are each a contrast of old native Moslem section and new Russian or russified section. An inhabitant of the largest, Tashkent (1,140,000), said that the ban on cattle in towns aroused more indignation there than anything for a decade. The Central Asian republics are separated from Siberia by the large Kazakh republic, which contains more Russians than Kazakhs; its capital, Alma-Ata (640,000), is in effect a Russian provincial town. In Siberia, which tends to regard itself as part of Europe, the larger towns are bunched in the Southern Urals

Dock porters in Odessa – notorious for their rudeness and neglect until tipped

and then stretch eastward to the Pacific, like rare beads on the single railway and its new spur lines, each an advance post of industrial wealth in the inhospitable climate. The largest, Novosibirsk (1,049,000), is mostly of one storey; it has a particularly active intellectual centre, partly because it is further from Moscow than any other very large Russian town.

A glimpse of life in Sverdlovsk (940,000), the Urals industrial centre, is given by a graduate engineer, a party member, who lives in a new housing estate there. He gets 150 rubles a month and his wife 50. They have three children and his mother-in-law, who looks after them more cheaply than a kindergarten. All the family's disposable income of 150 rubles is needed for food. Life is drab, with few places of entertainment and little leisure. He is up at 6 a.m. and home at 8 p.m., having to spend two and a half hours travelling to and from work. When he gets home he eats, watches television a little and goes to bed. There is no car in the entire estate but 'plenty where the bosses live'. The flats are not bad, 50 to a block. There are alcoholics in half the flats—it is incredible that there are so many, women as well as men. It starts from unhappiness and becomes a habit. Most of his neighbours do additional jobs, but some are on a starvation diet—for example a widow with two children who gets 50 rubles as a housing superintendent. She lives on bread, potatoes and a little milk and sugar. The instalment system made television sets possible, but these are now disliked because of the deductions from pay. Recent housing and food improvements are regarded as small compared with class differences. The local idols are workers with guts who insist on fairness, not the 'Heroes of Labour'. The rulers in Moscow are less disliked than the local bosses. The latter behaved typically in his factory when one of them took the last trade union pass to a sanatorium which should have gone to a sick forewoman. Everybody is for himself. Tatars and Mongols in the town are thought of as foreigners because of their poor Russian. (This description was given in 1966; the two female wages of 50 rubles would now be 60 rubles.)

Nearly half of the towns up to about 10,000 in population are classified as 'settlements of urban type'. Some are suburban or satellite extensions of large towns. Many are pioneer centres of industrial or transport development. Of the 22 million people who live in these settlements, those in the newer or more isolated ones certainly need a pioneering spirit. The families are mostly young, living in hostels and without a grandmother or crèche for the children when they arrive. Lack of schools causes many families to get out and their places are taken by villagers indentured on the promise of a passport. Conditions at a gold-mining 'settlement of urban type' in Siberia, just east of Lake Baikal, Rudnik Priiskovy, are described by a German who worked there after 10 years in a prison camp. At first, with cutlery and a waitress in the canteen, it was like a dream. Families had a room and kitchen in wooden barracks, but no running water or lavatory—a great difficulty in winter, leading to risk of typhoid in the spring. Many of the workers had received a sentence, not of detention but to live away from towns. Conditions were very hard, in snow and frequent blizzards eight months of the year. The woman doctor was more severe than the camp doctor had been in passing people fit for work. Wages were very high, up to 200 rubles a month for haulers, 140 for blasters and 250 for drillers. Many women worked there, as winch operators (80–100 rubles), haulers (100 rubles) and cleaners (32 rubles). Errors and quarrels in wage payment were very frequent. There was usually not enough cash for wages. The professional recruiters of labour for such settlements were called 'soul-catchers'. In one work group of 130, 200 left and as many arrived in one year. The manager got 800 rubles and chief engineer 500 rubles per month. They and other officials lived quite well. The machinery was good. Cave-ins were rare, but drillers tended to get silicosis, for which a life pension of 45–120 rubles was awarded.

For a single man to get his own room, the method was to move into a family's room and keep it after they left by threatening challengers with an axe. There were 1,700 inhabitants. Food supplies were good, even sugar and butter always being available. The staff of the four shops were intolerably rude unless the customer had good connections. Prices were not high—butter 2·85 rubles per kilogram, sugar 1·10, horse sausage one, around two for pork, cocoa nine, groats about 50 kopeks, bread 18 kopeks, vodka five rubles per litre and beer 25 kopeks a glass. The canteen was clean and a three-course meal cost 70–80 kopeks, consisting of the standard dishes served in all Soviet industrial and cheap public eating-places (beetroot-, cabbage- or rice-soup; cutlets, rissole or goulash; stewed fruit or jelly). As for clothing on sale, the German was stunned by its shoddiness even after 10 years in camp. The best suits were nearly 200 rubles and shoes 36 rubles, a wrist-watch 34 rubles, a bicycle 70–80 rubles. Furniture was atrocious and there was never children's shoes or nails. Social life was in separate groups: by nationality, the party clique and the professional thieves. Dances were popular, films twice a week, the usual library, 'Red corner' and political lectures, but very little political work by the Young Communist League. Fights were almost universal on the fortnightly pay-day, due to drink, and burglaries frequent. Law enforcement usually meant spending the nights in the jail and working as usual. Religion was of almost no importance, though many children were baptised, even of party parents, and icons were widespread. A priest came once a month. Some sects were active. Children up to 11 had a school and older ones boarded, returning for weekends. Young people read a great deal. Textbooks and other books were on sale even in the post-office. Most people spent all their wages quickly. Families tried to give their rooms individuality, in some cases by drawings on the wall and paper 'carpets'. All the crockery and cutlery on sale was identical; this was extraordinarily depressing. Couples teamed up quickly as those under sentence could be separated without warning. Some women had several children by different men—e.g. an Armenian, a Siberian Russian, a Tatar, a

German. There were seven small cars and five motor cycles in the settlement.

The conditions described are those of nearly 10 years ago. General improvements since must have affected the isolated or new 'settlements of urban type', but the higher wages might be less now, with the reduction since that time of preferential rates for occupations and areas of special difficulty. The conditions are, by and large, probably not very different at present for the large numbers of people in the many remote industrial settlements. The mine described has been worked for over a century and is equipped with American machinery. The prices given are, on the whole, slightly lower than those now prevailing in the big towns.

5

Some Occupations and Groups

The preceding chapters dealt with the general structure and circumstances of Soviet life. The remaining two chapters fill in the account with pen-pictures of groups, occupations and professions.

MANAGERS AND WORKERS

The canteens in a large factory are usually of three kinds: self-service and cheap for the workers, including grades up to foreman; cleaner and possibly with waitress service for the ITR (technical staff); distinctly better, with beer but not vodka available, for managerial staff. The director usually eats in his office suite. He has three chauffeurs (24 hours on and 48 off), two or three personal secretaries and usually two personal assistants. His pay, if the factory is engaged on special military production or is otherwise specially important, has virtually no limit, being 500–1,500 rubles a month basic plus very high bonuses depending on results. (The official regulations give 330 rubles as the maximum basic pay for a factory director.) The social-occupational levels in a sizeable factory are:

1. 'The works aristocracy', comprising the director, chief engineer, chief designer, the heads of the technology, mechanical and electrical departments, in metallurgical and certain other works the laboratory chief, the deputy directors for supply, for personnel, and for living conditions (plant housing and welfare). At a somewhat lower level are the heads of shops and of the finance, wages, despatch and book-keeping departments and the professional party leaders. The head of the 'Secret Department' (KGB) does not mix socially. The professional trade union leader at the plant may or may not be included. The main perquisite of these people is good housing, which the head of the capital construction department ensures. Most of the above, always including the director, are likely to be on the plant party committee (which will include some workers, who are paid for time

'We'll have to tell him again that it's oil'

spent at its meetings, and at least one woman). At, say, a banquet for important foreign visitors, the whole or upper part of this group will be present, sometimes with a few manual workers. At 'secret' plants, which are numerous, this level includes a number of military officers, who are paid from outside, but share in such plant perquisites as cars, good housing and free sanatoria passes.

2. Other managerial staff, the deputies of the 'aristocracy', any scientists who may be working in the laboratory, the heads of 'party cabinets' and senior technicians.

3. The ITR (graduate 'engineering-technical workers'). This may include foremen if they are graduates.

4. A large non-manual group, comprising between seven and 10 per cent of the entire staff: machine-setters, rate-fixers, materials allocators, inspectors, quality-control staff, controllers of various kinds.

5. Manual production workers, ranging from skilled men able to set their own machines to machine-minders: very varied in skill, with earnings ranging from about 70 to over 200 rubles. High earnings

invite piece-rate reductions. The more able workers are hated for this reason. If a man makes over 200–220 rubles in a month he is likely to ask for some of his pay chits to be held over and he will take time off in the next month. The average pay is well under 100 rubles. It is higher in military than civil production and in the big cities than the provinces.

6. Auxiliary workers, known as MOP ('junior servicing personnel'), numerous because of poor mechanisation. Loaders, internal transport (very poorly equipped), helpers (not responsible for work on machines —these are especially numerous), cleaners, watchmen, etc. The decree which raised minimum state pay from 40 to 60 rubles in 1968 was vital for this group, which has a very high proportion of women.

Except between the manual and non-manual levels, there are no very obvious differences in clothing. Certain kinds of safety clothing are issued free. The social distinctions are more marked in the provinces, where the 'aristocrats' are big fish, than in the large capital cities. The director's children will be at the local school (which may be attached to the factory), but it is easy for him to move them to a school of high reputation in another part of the town if he so wishes and his immediate subordinates can do the same. It is extremely rare for a woman or a non-party member to reach the industrial 'aristocracy', but there are many of both at the second level, and a large proportion of women at level 3 in factories which employ mainly female labour, but even in these men are predominant at level 4.

In the following we take a quick look at some industrial questions from the management's and worker's points of view.

Wages: The director can now, under the 1965 economic reform, decide within limits the proportions of different kinds and grades of labour, but still within his 'wages fund' which is set from above. He in no sense negotiates wage rates, which are established centrally for the industry as a whole. Every worker is graded by training and skill in six to eight grades, on which his wages—whether piece rates or time work—largely depend. All this is explained in the annual 'collective agreement' between the trade union and management, which also contains promises of better amenities from the management and better work from the workers, but has no other significance. Every worker gets a copy of the collective agreement. The test for a man's grade is a serious matter; disputes about it go to a shop disputes commission of trade union and management representatives.

The management can raise the general wage level by easing the tests, but will run into trouble with the local branch of the state bank if the wage fund is exceeded otherwise than by overfulfilment of plan. This is why the shop bookkeepers—in some factories at least—have a say in deciding grade tests. The higher amounts available for bonuses under the economic reform are being shared out unequally, partly to improve the relatively poor pay in level 3. By late 1967 in the engineering industries about 70 per cent of the bonus fund was going to levels 1–3 and 30 per cent to levels 4–6.

Dismissals: Managers are very reluctant to sack anybody as this can be done only on specified grounds, mainly infringement of discipline, and must be agreed by the trade union committee. A worker can appeal to the disputes commission, which usually upholds the dismissal, and he can then go to the labour session of the People's Court, which often reinstates him. Soviet economists have long said in private, and are now saying in public, that inability to dismiss staff is a serious hindrance to flexibility and technical progress. Redundancy is now officially recognised as proper grounds, under strict control, and redundancy allowances cover a fortnight to find another job, which is not difficult in the big industrial centres. In any case, it remains the director's responsibility to ensure that other jobs are available elsewhere for discharges due to redundancy. There is no unemployment pay and no labour exchanges, as the existence of unemployment is not officially admitted. The grounds for dismissal are entered in the labour book which every person in state employment carries. There is fuller information in a file which follows him from job to job and is kept by the management; this is distinct from the file which the KGB may have on him.

Trade unions: These are split, unofficially but in fact, between the workers' representatives, called *proforgs*, who are each responsible for the dues and problems of 15–20 of their comrades, and the trade union committee, in particular its full-time members, which tends to act, in general but not universally, as a branch of the management's personnel and wages departments. Higher up, the trade unions operate in effect as auxiliary personnel and wages departments of the respective industrial ministries. When ministries are divided or amalgamated, the same happens to the corresponding unions. Everybody in a factory is a member of the same union, except distinct sections such as the catering staff. Even the director is a member. There are few non-members, as the level of sickness and other benefits depends on membership. The trade unions are officially designated as 'schools of Communism' and 'transmission belts from the party to the masses'; in popular parlance they are called ticket agencies for sanatoria or, more briefly, travel agencies.

Strikes: These are illegal, not as strikes but as sabotage, and are matters for the KGB. They are never reported in the press. Since Stalin's death some strikes have developed into local riots and revolts. In recent years a flexible approach has developed; one strike leader was offered a very good post in another town, only to be quietly arrested a few months later. The result of a strike is likely to be dismissal or demotion of the management, party and trade union officials, arrest of the strike leaders and the more active strikers, intensified political work amongst the others and some local improvement of conditions. There are, however, so many informers amongst industrial workers that serious talk of going on strike is likely to bring about both arrests and concessions before any strike takes place.

Production propaganda: This is the primary task of the party and trade union committees. Every shop in a big factory has one or two full-time artists for this and associated political purposes. The director nominates a standing joint production committee which is rarely convened and has little significance. Campaigns are run for emulation between shops and factories for productivity red banners and other trophies, to which cash prizes are attached, but these work out at only about 10 rubles per man per quarter for the winners. Most of the productivity campaigns are ephemeral: since the revolution there have been about 300, of which the Stakhanovite movement in 1935 was the most publicised and long-lasting. The professional Young Communist League organiser in a factory is a kind of errand-boy for the party organisers in these matters; he and his committee have little influence on the young workers unless he shows himself to be useful in securing improvements in the factory hostel and in helping with job placements. The offices of the league in many factory towns are becoming, in effect, substitutes for the non-existent labour exchanges.

Vodka: The struggle by managements, party and trade unions for labour discipline is very largely a struggle against drunkenness. Fantastic and widely differing figures of chronic alcoholism in the Soviet industrial world are mentioned by Russians, but not published. There are strong traditions of drinking to initiate new workers and on many other occasions. Some directors in remote places set up illicit distilleries to keep their workers happy. As conditions improve, drink at work and absenteeism through drunkenness are said to be increasing instead of diminishing. The introduction of a five-day week in 1968 appears to have provided more time for drinking. During 1966–7 decrees were issued on the compulsory treatment of alcoholics of working age at their own expense. The 'Communist Brigades of Labour' undertake not to drink; this means abstention from vodka—they tend to be heavy drinkers of

The Nevsky Works in Leningrad

beer and wine. Even a 'non-drinker' in the Russian working class will take a quarter of a litre of vodka with a meal on Sundays.

Hours: Overtime is limited by law to 120 hours a year and may not be worked without the sanction of the trade union, which is usually given when the director requests it. He tries to avoid it, as overtime rates upset the wages plan. Overtime is not an important source of earnings. The working time is now 41 hours in a five-day week.

Idle time: This is more important to both director and workers than overtime. Unevenness of supply is a chronic complaint in industry. Production is too often dependent upon supplies 'from the wheel': a delayed vehicle may cause idle time. The effect of idle time on wages is not limited by the minimum wage law if the cause is judged to be the worker's fault.

Training and promotion: Training facilities are good and workers are strongly encouraged to make use of them in order to get a promotion of skill-grade. Workers may move up the social-occupational levels indicated above: from level 6 to level 5, and from 5 to 4—but in the latter case it often becomes necessary to join the party because production responsibility is involved. It is quite abnormal for workers, including foremen, to cross the line between levels 4 and 3. One way of doing this is to graduate in a technical subject by evening or correspondence courses—a most difficult undertaking, though good facilities are provided.

The economic reform: Decreed in 1965, this by now directly or indirectly affects all industrial managements. Few directors have gained much freedom to buy their inputs, which are mostly still allocated in the plan in specified quantities from specified warehouses or producers, at fixed prices. There is a little more relaxation in the relations between the manufacturers of consumer goods and the retail trade administrations. Directors are still instructed, but in less detail, with which others to make their inter-industry contracts and they are still liable to have to dishonour contracts because of new instructions from above. The new cost of production—a charge of around six per cent on capital—is compelling directors to use up hoarded stocks of inputs, but with little more confidence than hitherto in timely deliveries by suppliers. The reform was intended to abolish 'gross output' as the decisive criterion of performance, but ministries still appear to use it for evaluating the work of their enterprises. However, the new criterion is gaining ground: it is the value of output delivered to consignees and accepted by them. This new 'success indicator', together with a more serious attitude to costs which has been made possible by a rather limited reform of state prices, gives more meaning to profits. A substantial proportion of profits is now left at the disposal of the director in running his enterprise and a smaller but important proportion is available for amenities and for distribution as bonuses. Soviet industry, with labour protected by the laws controlling dismissal, is very heavily overstaffed at all levels. As cost criteria become more sophisticated, further development of the reform will probably involve unemployment and less central regulation of wages. But the government may find it socially too dangerous and thus politically impossible to modify the security of employment and ease of getting a new job which have become a traditional expectation of the working class. This is a critical obstacle to general relaxation of central controls over economic managers. The other main obstacle is the industrial bureaucrats, whether in the ministries, the state banking system, the party town and province offices or those directors who are so accustomed to the rigidities of the 'command economy' that they cannot administer a more flexible system. For nearly 40 years they and their predecessors have worked on the simple principle operated by the planners and the ministries of increasing the output of everything by a certain percentage each year, whether the output was required or not and without real concern for cost. (There are odd results of the new stress on profits as the economic reform spreads beyond industry. The gas, electricity and water in the campers' kitchen of a tourist camp were cut off or made unusable during August 1968. A surmise that this was done in order to compel people to use the camp restaurant and thus increase profits was confirmed.)

PUSHERS AND PLANNERS

The Russian dictionary's definition of *tolkach* is: 'One who gives a push, speeds up business necessary at the moment but sometimes without concern for the general, planned course of work and infringing it.' The Soviet economy is characterised by two opposite but complementary types: the planner and the tolkach. Both are essential. Without the planners a factory director would not know what to produce, while his tolkachi (pushers) enable him to produce it. Ideally, the planners arrange for materials, subcontractors, machinery, finance, labour, customers, costs, prices, profits or losses and every-thing else of importance. In practice, business life is, more than in the unplanned economies, a series of crises. Factories send out their tolkachi, not to get orders but to get supplies or expedite their transport—although these have already been planned, authorised and allocated. This is often true even of the key factories which are most fully looked after by the planners. The economic reform of 1965 was intended to make both bureaucratic planning and energetic pushing less paramount in the economy, but so far it has had little effect. A good tolkach is a very distinctive type—invaluable to his director, wise in the ways of the Soviet business world, with innumerable connections, a master of *blat* (wire-pulling, mutual services, influence and threats—up to bribery and blackmail—to get things done). Planners are not less practical in their own sphere, but their sphere is very different: a world of quantities on paper, which have to fit. Information on the production, transport, transfer, quality, etc. of the quantities must be on standardised forms, for otherwise the billions of elements in the economy cannot be fitted together to form the plan. These forms are, necessarily, more real to the planners than the factories and their problems. Planners are not less doughty in this paper world (in which, for example, between seven and nine million state prices are set and coordinated) than tolkachi are in theirs. The author would like to suggest to a Russian novelist or film producer a drama of rivalry between a master tolkach and a master planner for the hand of a female factory director. Other types, from the local state bank or party bureau for example, would appear as minor characters in this titanic situation.

WOMEN

The burden of Soviet economic growth has rested heavily on the shoulders of women, amongst the Russians more than other Soviet nations. Full-time housewives of working age (up to 55) are rare, except in the Russian upper middle and upper classes and in all classes of the non-Russian republics. The proportion of all Soviet women at work in the main child-bearing and child-rearing age group (20–40) is 80 per cent, but it is up to 90 per cent in the Russian working and lower middle classes and around 70–80 per cent in the other republics. Nearly three-quarters of all women in the 41–54 age group and about half of those aged 55–64 are at work. Homes with children are run to a considerable extent by widowed grandmothers. There is one place in a crèche or kindergarten for every four children of pre-school age in the towns, and minding facilities for a similar proportion during the intensive summer work in the villages. These pre-school institutions in the towns are not, in general, of a high standard. Middle-class mothers avoid them and they cost enough to be avoided by the working class: 10–15 rubles a month for a child is normal. Much depends on the place of work: a well-run factory in the more modern section of the textile industry is likely to provide good care for children and facilities for nursing mothers; some such factories take children 24 hours a day for the entire working week.

The housewife's work is lightened, in some respects, by having to look after only one or two rooms, or a very small flat in the new housing. But shopping to feed a family is a strategic operation, involving a search for particular items even in the largest towns. The strain on the working wife or the older retired woman is very great. Working-class husbands show little inclination to help, though social habits are changing in this respect. There has been much talk ever since the 1920s of rationalising housekeeping by the sale of prepared foodstuffs and semi-cooked meals; in this, however, the USSR remains a long way behind other industrial countries, where such conveniences have developed without fuss in response to consumer demand. In the Russian towns there is a tendency to get by with a minimum of cooking.

'I promise to build crèches' – a stock subject of humorous drawings in the 1960s

A study of time budgets amongst adults in full-time employment in some towns of Krasnoyarsk province shows the time spent by men over 25 years of age on household tasks, including allotments, as 25 hours a week. For employed women aged 25–50 it is 45 hours. For employed women over 50 it is 55 hours, the increase being due mostly to more time spent on the allotment.

Women are employed on heavy work in factories, on the railways and at building sites. Working women constitute just over half the state-employed labour force, but the great majority of them are in the least skilled, least desirable and lowest-paid occupations. In the conditions of very uneven mechanisation the manual work has to be done by somebody; working-class women do it because they have to supplement their husbands' wages for the family to eat. In the working class men also have far more access to the training courses and other opportunities for the better jobs. This is why so many women can be seen doing such work as handling materials manually in construction (an industry in which they form 28 per cent of the labour force). There is plenty of legislation on female labour, forbidding night work and heavy, dangerous or underground work, but entire industries employing almost solely female labour work 24 hours a day under an exemption clause. The average pay of all women in state employment was probably about half that of men before the minimum wage was raised from 40 to 60 rubles in January 1968.

Once they get out of the working class by a higher education,

A woman wielding a heavy pneumatic drill in a Moscow street

women have broad but limited opportunities. Nearly three-quarters of all doctors and a third of the graduate engineers are women. In such 'mass professions' relatively few of them reach directing posts or earn much more than a moderately skilled male worker. There are women students in the defence, KGB and diplomatic higher training institutions, but on a low quota. Intellectual Russian women consider this quota disgraceful. Discussions on sex equality usually come round to the same conclusion: equality depends not only on opportunity but also on material conditions like public transport, shops, housing and washing machines, and on a level of culture in which one does not have to fight one's way on to an overcrowded tram. The women are liable to be exhausted before they get to work in the morning. In public life a large proportion of members of the soviets are women (consistently just over a quarter in the USSR Supreme Soviet and just over two-fifths at all levels of the local soviets) because the party officials responsible for arranging the composition of these almost powerless bodies work to such a plan. The party bureaus have few women members at any level. Only one woman has ever reached the Politbureau, and she did not stay in it long. The exercise of political power, or of administrative authority, tends to be a rather more harsh occupation in the USSR than in more relaxed social systems, and women are not good at it. In addition, the hangover of traditional peasant attitudes to women as sharers of the hard work but not of decision-making is much stronger

in Russia than in more evolved countries, and stronger still in
most of the other Soviet republics. In the writer's opinion Soviet
women are more orthodox and dogmatic than men in intellectual
occupations.

As in other fields, policy and legislation on family matters have
changed very sharply several times. Divorce and abortion, which
were very easily available until 1936, were made very difficult to
obtain in that year and divorce was made almost impossible in 1944.
Abortion was made legal and easy again in 1955, partly because of the
very high rate of illegal and dangerous operations, and divorce is now
again easy to obtain. Both are resorted to very widely. In 1966 the
Soviet divorce rate became higher than the American—2·8 per
thousand of the population as against 2·5—after a further relaxation
of the divorce laws in 1965. An abortion every year is not uncommon,
and there are more legal abortions than live births, as well as many
illegal ones still. A recent Soviet novel depicts an explosion of
anger amongst women living in a factory hostel who are fed up with
the repeated abortions made necessary by the impossibility of
rearing children there. Contraceptives have never been widely
available or very reliable; their production is being improved in an
attempt to reduce the number of abortions, which impose a heavy
burden on the hospitals. The government is concerned at the
present very steep fall in the birth-rate, but cannot possibly resort to
the prohibitions of 1936 and 1944 in the present temper of public
opinion. There are no books on sex for adults, and only the beginnings
of instruction in the schools on human reproduction.

Working mothers are helped by maternity leave of eight weeks
before birth and at least eight weeks after, normally on full pay.
Family allowances are complicated: a lump sum at birth, ranging
from 20 rubles for the third child to 85 for the fifth (it rises to 250
rubles for the eleventh living child) plus a monthly payment of
four rubles for the fourth child rising to 15 rubles for the eleventh.
The monthly payments stop at the child's fifth birthday: thus payments are unlikely to be made for more than four children at a time,
however large the family. What this amounts to is, for example,
133 rubles for five children, two of them under five, in the year of the
fifth child's birth. (A British mother of five children would get £176
a year, for a very much longer period.) Unmarried mothers in the
USSR receive additional children's allowances, as a right and not as a
relief concession: five rubles a month for the first child, 7½ rubles for
the second and 10 rubles for the third, until 12 years of age. An

unmarried mother also has the legal right to place her child or children in an institution and to take them back when she so wishes. Illegitimacy remains a social though not an official stigma. In addition to cash, mothers of large families receive the Motherhood Medal, second class, for a fifth living child and first class for a sixth, the Order of Motherhood Glory (three classes) for a seventh, eighth or ninth, and the title 'Heroine Mother' for a tenth. The lists of awards in the official gazette show them as going predominantly to Moslem women. Family allowance money goes mainly to these women and to the village women of other nations.

Alimony is payable, up to half of a man's wages for three or more children, deducted by his employer. Fatherhood out of wedlock bears no financial responsibility. *De facto* marriage was at one time recognised in law and still is in some respects. The draft of a new law on marriage issued in April 1968 proposes to restore paternal responsibility for illegitimate children, but only if the parents cohabited; in other respects the draft abolishes recognition of *de facto* marriage. This draft law also gives much attention to marriage between Soviet citizens and foreigners, which at one time was banned by law and is still made very difficult in practice.

Prostitution does not exist in the USSR so far as the official ideology is concerned, and there are therefore no published laws or regulations concerning it. The word *prostitutka* is often used of a 'good-time' girl with no other connotation, especially one who associates with foreigners. The number of women who make a living by prostitution is small compared with the number who, in the circumstances of Soviet employment, earn something extra or get favoured treatment at work by this means. The number of professional prostitutes exiled from the large towns to remote places under the law against parasites (people without jobs) in the early 1960s was sufficient to cause outcries from the local women loud enough to reach the central newspapers when the exiles descended on their husbands. There are sophisticated prostitutes who may be termed official, being employed to contact foreigners in whom the KGB are interested. Students use the term 'honest giver' for female fellow-students who do not ask payment for intercourse.

MOTORISTS

Soviet motor-car owners visiting Western countries are particularly impressed by the plethora of petrol stations and repair services. There

Coping with traffic signals – 'This is the only place I can drop you'

are now about 100,000 private car owners in Moscow and several times that number in the whole country. Petrol stations are still rather rare; in an attempt to stop the purchase of fuel from lorry drivers private motorists have been submitted to bureaucratic controls (such as having to prove that their legal purchases of fuel correspond to their mileage) which are recognised as excessive even by Soviet standards. Minor repairs are granted as a concession, often with the aid of a bribe, because the few garages fulfil their plans, which are based on value of turnover, more conveniently by replacing entire engines or gearboxes. Minor spare parts are scarce in any case. Moscow has 11 servicing garages, which work mostly on official cars. Owners who are engineers with access to equipment enjoy doing their own maintenance and even making replacements, but others face many tribulations. Car mechanics are kings. They accept up to a dozen vehicles at 30–50 rubles a month each for maintenance in their spare time, charging extra for replacements which they obtain by devious means. Private cars are laid up for the winter and undergo an official test in the spring. The conditions for a driving licence include fairly strict standards of physical fitness and some mechanical knowledge. It is easy to lose one's licence for several years by traffic misdemeanours, especially drink: the tests for alcohol are often arbitrary and crude. A friend of the writer whose application for insurance became bureaucratically bogged drove for a year without any insurance whatever.

Despite all difficulties, since the 1930s, when car production began, the convenience and fascination of owning a car have been a beacon to many who can afford the cost. Above all, people want the feeling of independence and privacy that a car can provide. Roads between some of the main towns in the western part of the European area, and within the largest of these towns, are good. Road markings and route signs are, however, primitive, in contrast to the numerous expensive heroic statues and political signs such as GLORY TO THE CPSU and THE PARTY AND THE PEOPLE ARE ONE. The interest in cars is visible in the admiring small crowds which collect around new American models. Production has run at about 200,000 a year (compared with between one and two million in Western European countries and Japan, and nine million in the United States), mostly for official use and subsidised export. The waiting lists of private customers became unmanageable by the middle 1950s and led to a variety of ingenious illegal activities. The lists were closed for seven years and, when they were reopened, prices were raised steeply.

Customers had to present testimony that the money had been acquired honestly. But the silent pressure continued and became an unacknowledged political issue between the middle class and the government, which was not only unwilling to put resources into this industry, it was worried at the freedom of movement and transport, with its consequences for unofficial commercial and political activities, that extensive ownership of private vehicles would make possible.

The post-Khrushchev government appears to have given way on this difficult issue. Foreign firms, mainly Fiat, have been invited to help set up a modern motor-car industry and the current five-year plan aims at an output of 800,000 vehicles a year by 1970. It is not yet clear whether the Soviet middle class has achieved much of a victory in this matter: the result will depend on the proportion of vehicles sold to them, as distinct from the number exported. Present prices are high: about 4,500 rubles for a medium-powered car of indifferent quality, built to cope with very bad roads. Petrol is cheap. The number of new cars sold has been steady at about 50,000 a year for the past seven or eight years in the towns and has risen in the country-side from 7,000 to 19,000 in that period. Traffic is becoming heavy in the largest towns. It consists of lorries, buses and official cars; light vans, private cars and taxis are few in number.

HOLIDAY-MAKERS

The ordinary Soviet citizen on holiday is either organised or 'wild'—i.e. either with a group, usually under trade union auspices, or making his own arrangements. The organised kind numbered 17 million in 1965; about half of these were children in summer camps under educational and Young Communist League auspices. Of the organised adults, most stay in institutions of a loosely medical character; they do physical exercises in the early morning and lie down for an hour in the after-noon. In addition, tourist

Moscow: examining a foreign car

camps are being increasingly used for organised holidays: the groups which stay in them alternate excursions with 'socially useful work' such as helping with the local harvest. Sharing out sanatoria or camp holiday tickets, which are subsidised, is a principal function of the trade union branches. 'Wild' holiday-makers are greatly increasing in number with the growth of money incomes.

ATHLETES

The Soviet statistical abstract for 1965 gives 46·3 million as the number of 'physical culturists' and 48,800 masters of sport. The two figures illustrate the two aims of the state in its financing and planning of sport since the war: maximum active participation, and spectator sport. The latter involves a system of star teams and performers which serves a third aim—international prestige. The link between mass participation and the star system is the figure of 8,257,000 holders of the designation 'graded sportsman'. This is made up of 103,000 first grade, 735,000 second, 3,470,000 third and 3,949,000 youth grade. There is a most elaborate grading system for attainments in every kind of sport, athletics and games. All this has a special place in Soviet society: the political and the ordinary human interests come together in sport perhaps more closely than in any other sphere. The state wants everybody to be 'Ready for Labour and Defence' (the award for fitness and sports prowess, under this name, was gained by 70 million people in the 30 years up to 1960); it also wants the USSR to be top nation in all sports. The Soviet public have

On the beach at Sochi, a popular resort

the same desire as the people of any other country for activity, excitement and patriotic victories. Perhaps the popular interest in sport is even stronger than in other countries because of the special need for non-political release of tension. Also, leisure tends to be spent outside the home because of cramped housing conditions. Talent is spotted at the schools and in the 200,000 local and sectional sports clubs. None of the sports clubs is independent of the party, which exercises control in this field mainly through the Young Communist League, the trade unions and the all-embracing Union of Sports Societies and Organisations. The two largest of the national sports clubs are those of the army and the KGB (which sponsors the predominant Dynamo club). The sports staff is immense; it includes 2,200 doctors who specialise in this sphere.

Large cash awards for record achievements, nominal posts at high salaries, permanent training facilities and many perquisites are the rewards of outstanding performers, which in effect makes them professionals rather than amateurs. Amongst the most eagerly sought rewards is to be on the list for trips abroad; the possibility of not going abroad again if one does not do well in an international competition is a very strong inducement to do well. Soviet teams abroad

Lenin Stadium, the Moskva river and Moscow University

have much to put up with from the political controllers accompanying them, who may know nothing about the particular field of sport or athletics but have the responsibility of ensuring victory and preventing defection. However, like scientists, the professional in Soviet sport has the inner happiness of being able to apply his skill more or less single-mindedly, without having to protect or betray its standards all the time, as is the case in many other fields of special endeavour, because the full exercise of his expertise is in line with what the party wants.

NATIONAL CADRES

As soon as the Baltic states of Latvia, Lithuania and Estonia had been firmly taken over by the USSR at the end of the Second World War, the Soviet political police searched out persons who were or had been active or influential in political and intellectual life. They were divided into those usable as 'national cadres' through whom the Soviet system could be implanted and those not; the latter were got rid of by various means, including death and deportation. (The most intensive operation of this kind occurred in Riga in one night of 1946; the rumours say that 80,000 people were taken away.) Other natives were in due course selected, for example young people to be trained as socialist realist writers in their own languages by the Union of Soviet Writers. In Lithuania the local Communist Party, thus reconstructed, proved incapable of introducing the collective farm system or of coping with the influx of Russian and Byelorussian peasants in search of a pre-collective life. So the KGB took this over, by deporting large numbers of the Lithuanian farmers and then offering the rest the straight alternatives of deportation or joining collective farms.

By the early 1950s the armed revolts against collectivisation were crushed and the Soviet system was firmly implanted, with its local KGB, Communist Party, governments and soviets, legal system, Young Communist League, trade unions, industrial system, press and radio and censorship, schools, universities and technical colleges, political schools, atheist propaganda societies and controls over the churches, professions, arts, sports organisations and voluntary social bodies. All these are guided and run by a combination of native cadres and Russians; the latter are still in charge in the key sectors, though often acting as deputy heads. In the past 10–15 years the system has settled in sufficiently for the peculiarities of the three Baltic nations to shape, in various minor ways, the Soviet process of

A member of the high-jump team

rapid industrial and educational growth, and to a lesser extent intellectual life, within the very tight framework.

The whole process is a recapitulation of the way in which the non-Russian areas of the old Empire were brought within the Soviet system after the Bolshevik government had won the civil war in 1920. But that process was naturally slower; it went parallel with the changes of problem, policy and method in Russia itself, in the course of construction and modification of the Soviet system as we now know it. One wave after another of national cadres was selected, placed in positions of pseudo-power, eliminated and replaced. The usual grounds for elimination were 'bourgeois nationalism'. The few national cadres who reached the Politbureau in Moscow were mostly so russified as to be more Russian than the Russians (Stalin, from an earlier generation of the party, is the dominating example). Jews are the outstanding exception in the whole process: they did not respond to the offer of an area in Eastern Siberia in which to settle and have national cadres; instead, they have played a prominent part in the

construction and manning of the system itself in Russia proper and
other republics, but are now excluded from the key sectors of it.
(This exclusion is facilitated by the internal passport, in which the
nationality of the holder is inscribed. One of the jokes at the time of
Khrushchev's defeat of his opponents in the Politbureau in 1957 was
that he had treated them too leniently: he should have put 'Jew' in
their passports and then let them try to get jobs. The situation in
1968 was summed up fairly enough by a Jewish engineer who said:
'We are not pushed into the ground but we are always under suspicion.' The most usual forms of discrimination seem to be blocked
promotion, being kept at the end of housing queues and being kept
out of the better universities and colleges.)

While all this has been going on, the usual process, visible in every
'backward' part of the world, of self-identification in terms of language, culture, religion, history, local soil and scenery, etc., has been
affecting the less developed peoples of the USSR, including their
national cadres. At the same time, the opposite or complementary
process of cultural influence by the more advanced nations has also
been evident within the Soviet system, reinforced—generally speaking—by the power of the state which regards the Russian nation as,
in principle, superior to all others. Russian people have, in full
measure, the sense of special national worth usually found in innovat-
ing nations. But the feeling is a mixed one: there is in it a sense of
inferiority, in relation to the culture of Western and Central Europe
and the technology of the United States. The contradiction is sometimes evident in the behaviour of Russians who stand behind the
national cadres in the Baltic republics.

National cadres were also implanted by the USSR in most of the
formally independent countries of Eastern Europe after the Second
World War, and copies of the Soviet system were established through
them. When these cadres were overthrown by the Hungarians in
1956 they were installed again with the aid of the Soviet army. (The
writer, who was in Prague when the Russians invaded in August
1968, cannot visualise national cadres being installed again in
Czechoslovakia—short of incorporating the country in the USSR and
decimating its population.) Many of the political emigres from the
non-Russian republics of the USSR believe that their nations will, in
due course, do the same despite—or because of—the great stimulation
of their industrial and educational advance under Stalin and his
successors. This question is made more complicated by the very great
difference of development between the smaller western and eastern

republics of the USSR. Latvia and Estonia, for example, are in the same world as Scotland and Wales while Tajikstan and Turkmenia are—except for the Russians living there—more similar, at least in their peasantries, to the neighbouring Iran and Afghanistan.

INFORMERS

Soviet life is poisoned by the system of informers who are recruited, often under threat, by the political police (now called the KGB). Before the war the political police boasted of 100 million eyes and ears. Its vast network of informers was probably the chief source of its frequent regular reports to the Politbureau on the mood of the population. In the circumstances of that time the sheer size of the informer network must

On the road from Alma-Ata to Frunze

have contributed to the extent of the great purge. The network is still enormous. The following is a translation of some rules that were recently compiled by a Soviet official who has for many years been an unwilling informer.

How to recognise informers

1   They are somewhat independent in relation to superiors.
2   They use other telephones, leaving the work-place suddenly without explanation, to report at a precise time.
3   They are arrogant and nosey, doing their own work badly.
4   They grumble against the leadership or praise it highly without honest reasons.
5   They may propose illegal deals, black market operations, etc.
6   They go silent in political conversation (listening hard) which they themselves have stimulated.
7   They mostly render little disinterested help to others.
8   Look for an informer if the boss changes his attitude to you: he may have received a communication from the KGB.

9   They sometimes phone without saying the name of the person called.

10   The KGB uses other nationalities—e.g. Jewish informers on Russians; non-Ukrainian KGB officials in the Ukraine, etc. The unhappy (isolated) position of Jews makes them easier to recruit.

How to behave in relation to the KGB

1   Look happy. Be considerate to all, even known informers, and to them especially.

2   Remember, in relations with women, that they are more dangerous informers than men.

3   Tell a known informer what you want him to tell the KGB.

4   If a known informer is against you, use other informers to counteract him.

5   Create an impression of having protectors—the informer's attitude will be respectful.

6   Make no hasty statements.

7   Be especially careful with stupid people who believe the press and radio.

8   Distrust morally corrupt people—they are likely to be used by the KGB.

9   Be especially vigilant when asked about other people.

How to behave as an informer

1   Remember you are watched, like anybody else.

2   To identify your watcher, watch the place for your meeting with the KGB man so as to see who else meets him.

3   Remember that often the KGB man tears up your 'diligent' reports.

4   There is plenty of scope for helping, and much more for not harming, your assigned people, if done sensibly—especially in writing 'characterisation' reports on your friends and correspondents.

5   But remember that these reports are used for checking on you, too.

6   No KGB official can be trusted.

7   The KGB get rid (by imprisonment, etc.) of long-service informers who may know too much.

8   Put 'ideas' in the heads of KGB men. (This man used to invent reports of what foreigners had said to him, when he knew that other informers could not check such reports, along such lines as:

Local officials, Lithuanian Republic, 1959. Left to right (standing): *(1) head of agricultural department, county party bureau; (2) head of industry department, town party bureau; (3) director of meat-packing combine, formerly Deputy Minister of Meat and Dairy Procurements in another small republic; (4) head of the 'organisation department' of town party bureau; (sitting): (5) chairman of a collective farm; (6) senior mechanic at the same farm. The first three trusted each other fully, but were careful with the fourth, whose post is semi-KGB, and the fifth, an informer. The sixth, pleasant and reliable, had no political status. The first and third are Russians, the second and fourth Ukranians, the fifth and sixth Lithuanians*

'Communism and atheism are a religion which defends the ruling group.')

9   Higher KGB men think themselves important, but are only tools of the top. Some KGB men have 'personal' informers to protect themselves, but this is risky for them.

10 The KGB breaks up personal friendships which are dangerous to the system by, e.g., stimulating mutual denunciations.

11 If you are the head of an organisation, try to foster goodness in your subordinates, including the informers amongst them.

12 An anonymous letter, in disguised handwriting and with no fingerprints, can help a friend whom you know to be in danger or buttress his morale.

13   If the KGB asks you to worm your way into somebody's confidence, quarrel with him in order to avoid this.

Relations between people are not a simple matter in any modern society. The additional complication in Soviet society caused by the informer system, especially in the sphere of friendship and mutual trust, makes the whole country ill in a sense that may or may not be definable by social psychologists or psychiatrists, but is real enough to the inhabitants.

CRIMINALS

There are, in effect, three kinds of criminal in the USSR: political, economic and ordinary. The first type is a consequence of the many laws designed to protect the system of government and its ideas. In the 1930s the proportion of the adult population arrested or sentenced for alleged political crimes was at least a twentieth and possibly a tenth. Twenty years later Khrushchev claimed that conviction for political offences had ceased. No such claim could be made in the middle 1960s, when arrests for political and ideological reasons increased. Those arrested include people who make or organise protests against actions of the authorities and determined members of such religious congregations as are not officially licensed to exist. In early 1968 rumour in the USSR put the number in prisons, prison camps and asylums on political and religious grounds at a million, but this is probably an exaggeration.

Economic crime is a consequence of the illegality of private enterprise and the fact that people steal and embezzle state property with no very strong sense of doing wrong. It is, for example, a criminal offence to buy goods in order to sell them at a higher price, but this is done by so many people that it helps to even out the planners' deliberate or unintended inequalities of supply between different areas and periods. Indignant reports appear in the press from time to time of illegal small factories making goods not provided by the state, using purloined machines and materials and selling the products at great profit, the main cost of production being vast sums for bribery. In the period 1961–4 several hundred death sentences were reported for economic crimes. Inside the USSR in mid-1968 absurd estimates were current on the number of people in prison for economic offences. The writer was given a figure of 18 million by a doctor, as a piece of hard information. Such fantasies indicate what otherwise responsible people are prepared to believe on this subject—i.e. their estimate of the extent of illegal economic activity. The extent is certainly far greater than in the writer's previous experience of the USSR. It would probably be difficult to find many people who are not making something extra by illegal or illicit means.

The remaining group would be regarded as criminals anywhere. Statistics in this field are not published, since crime is regarded in the official theory as merely a declining hangover from capitalism or due to the corrupting influence of foreign capitalism. The number of thefts, assaults and murders has, however, always been great because of the poverty and strain in Soviet life, the number of people on the move and the brutalising effect of war and of harsh administration. The most professional and highly organised part of the Soviet criminal world amounts almost to a social order of its own: its members (at least until the middle 1950s) solemnly renounced certain elements of normal citizenship such as holding a job, marriage, singing the Soviet anthem and service in the armed forces. Their local organisations held national conferences from time to time: at such a gathering shortly after the German invasion it was decided not to steal from men in the forces.

Conditions for convicted criminals vary considerably. The main element in Soviet theory on the function of imprisonment is that society, the state and Communism must be protected by isolating persons who endanger them. It is also a Marxist principle that such persons are not innately wicked, since nobody is, but have been distorted by bad influences or conditions and should be given every possibility of reform through re-education and work. One of the many social organisations in the USSR is the prison commissions of local citizens who visit prisoners, receive their complaints and assist in their education. A craftsman employed in a small Soviet prison as a foreman and teacher of his trade, recently asked by the writer about conditions there, dwelt on the fact that the prison governor was successful in keeping the output plan low so as to avoid underfulfilment. Pressed to describe the place as a *prison*, he did not think the conditions very different from any small factory, apart from the people being locked up. In the early 1930s the reform-by-work idea developed into the vast and murderous system of labour camps. These have not been completely dismantled, but the conditions have improved almost beyond recognition.

One such camp has been described by a foreigner who was imprisoned there from 1961 to 1967 for a currency offence. It is in a group of 14 camps, officially known as *Dubrovlag*, about 200 miles south-east of Moscow, in the Potma-Yavas-Barashevo area, with a total of some 12,000 prisoners. Two of the camps are for women only, and a small one is for foreigners and stateless persons. Several are for political offenders: the inmates of one of these are known as 'the tigers' because of their striped prison uniform. One camp holds mostly Baptists, Jehovah's Witnesses and members of certain Russian religious sects. (The writers Yuli Daniel and Andrei Sinyavsky and the Englishman Gerald Brooke were in this set of camps at the time of writing.) In general, political and religious offenders are subject to stricter discipline than the ordinary convicts.

The four types of discipline described in this set of camps are:

1   'General regime': normal work with pay, barrack housing, free movement within the camp; correspondence with immediate relatives permitted; 10 rubles a month may be spent in the camp shop, one parcel a month allowed and one 'private visit' in six months (i.e. three full days with husband or wife in special quarters within the camp).

2   'Strengthened regime': harder work, seven rubles a month may be spent and one parcel received every three months; correspondence as above; one private visit in six months, but the prisoner works during the three days of the visit.

3   'Strict regime': heavy or dangerous work; five rubles may be spent and one letter sent per month; no private visits, but one visit of four hours per year; parcels—none, or one each four months.

4   'Very strict': striped uniform; very hard work (e.g. stone quarries); two rubles per month may be spent, one letter per year written and no visitors received.

The conditions described above by this former prisoner are, in principle, as laid down by the published regulations, except that the 'very strict' discipline is legally intended only for 'malicious' and recidivist offenders and for those reprieved from a death sentence. In 1963 a fifth type of camp regime was introduced in some places, without bars or guarded fences, the prisoners moving freely inside and outside the camp and usually employed in the local forestry or other enterprises. In Stalin's time the political police ran research institutes to employ imprisoned scientists, as well as extensive industries. In order to ensure secrecy in new military technology after the war, people working on it were put under a formal prison regime. Thus some aircraft designers worked in convict uniform. In the case of rocket engineers, prison-type discipline was also used to prevent them wasting time on what were then regarded by the authorities as space fantasies.

THE INTELLIGENTSIA

An *intelligent* (pronounced with a hard g) in late Tsarist Russia was a thoughtful person, deeply and uncompromisingly concerned with large moral and political issues, devoted to the common good and often also to the 'light of science'; usually of good social position, highly educated and very radical. There are various Russian words which denote opposite or very different kinds of person or outlook. Some of them are usually translated as 'philistine': their meanings connote narrow concern with one's own problems or with feasible comfort, an attitude of couldn't-care-less, or mundane business and practicality. The Bolshevik leaders were primarily intelligenti from the professional and minor aristocratic classes and educated Jewry. They had a practical streak and a supreme self-confidence—derived from Marxism as the immutable science of society—which enabled them to seize power when the aristocracy was in disarray, the business community not sufficiently homogeneous or mature for resolute action, and other sections of the political intelligentsia too self-doubting. They kept power by exercising another strand in the intelligentsia tradition—unrestricted sacrifice of everything for the common good. But they released the social revolution; under Stalin they were replaced by men from the masses who mistrusted all intelligenti, but took over traces of Communist ideals and the readiness to sacrifice, while interpreting the common good as power, industrial and military for Russia and, in effect, personal power for themselves. The new men interpreted the Marxist crusade against 'the blind forces of the market' as a need to control everything.

These people overdid it. Under Khrushchev the wheel came full circle, with his 'goulash Communism' as the new philistinism, and now a reappearance of something like the old intelligenti, mainly amongst the young people educated since Stalin. For these new intelligenti the letter translated in Chapter 1 would be intolerable, as *pretending* to condemn philistinism while in fact expressing the desire of its author for the comfort of undisturbed faith at the expense of honesty and reason. Glimpses of the new intelligentsia are appearing in the world's press, as authors of books published abroad or as younger people sentenced for circulating transcripts of the trials of such authors. Honesty in literature and the right to genuine information form a focus of their aspirations. They obtain and disseminate uncensored information and organise illegal gatherings at which uncensored poetry is declaimed. It is possible that, unlike their predecessors under the last Tsars, who provided leaders for all the political parties and all spheres of thought, they have no political significance for the future. They do not have much chance against the KGB with its masses of informers. The fact that eminent scientists are now (1968) beginning to protest openly at the more flagrant abuses of power may, however, help them. They have no vehicle of revolutionary self-confidence remotely comparable with the Marxism of their Bolshevik predecessors.

Nothing is known of any contact between people of this kind and the working class—which may now mistrust *intelligentiki* even more than its peasant grandfathers and great-grandfathers did. They tend to be regarded in all classes as strange, irresponsible and—worst of all—unpatriotic, perhaps because of the relatively large number of Jews amongst them. (In Russia proper, Tsarist or Soviet, ethnic patriotism has always been the real religion.) All the same, elements of the intelligentsia attitude or personality are far more widespread than the people who can be regarded as the new intelligenti. One finds touches of it in the most ordinary people, even in those who can properly be called philistines, and even in vicious brutes. It is part of the Russian make-up. Russian Communism has, in all its phases, been some kind of expression of it—even while the surviving intelligentsia was being destroyed in the great purge.

THE GENERATIONS

Many of the elderly people in the upper reaches of Soviet public and professional life owe everything to the Soviet regime. As proletarian party 'activists' of very poor education, they were given preferential places in the new technical and political colleges during the 1930s and replaced the generation of party and professional men destroyed in the great purge. The present Prime Minister, Kosygin, who was born in 1904, is the most eminent of this generation and type. More typical is the late head of a republic academy of architecture, a stupid man of peasant stock, aware of his professional incompetence and complete lack of polish. His salary was 1,000 rubles a month and he liked to say, most sincerely and accurately,

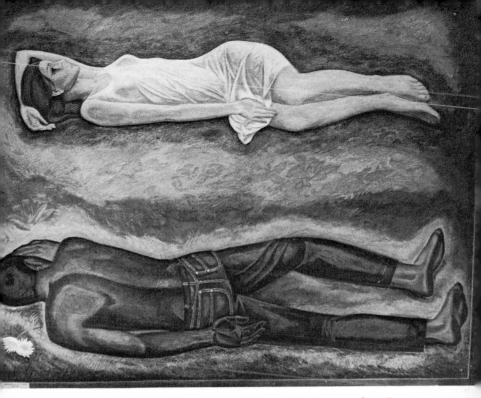

'The Couple' by Popkov. Shown in exhibitions of Soviet art abroad, it is unusually advanced for a Soviet painting

that only the Soviet power could have given him such an opportunity in life. He was completely loyal and devoted to the party. He loved to buy exotic things on trips abroad: a pair of lilac slippers would 'make Kiev gape'. Another such, who died recently, was a woman born in 1900 of landless peasant parents: she worked devotedly for the party in the Central Russian provinces during the 1920s, then graduated from the Institute of Red Professorship and from 1949 to her death was head of the principal centre providing refresher courses for teachers of Marxism-Leninism in higher education. More innocent than the architect and a better person, she retained her Communist faith through everything and could not understand sophisticated doubts. The letter in Chapter 1 would express her views, but she lacked the education and ability to formulate them. (The letter was from another Russian woman professionally engaged in Marxism-Leninism, over 20 years younger, belonging to a rather more sophisticated generation.) These two people, working in

Young people dancing in a café

architecture and education, were not brutalised by power, like many of their contemporaries who otherwise are very similar to them.

What kind of people are taking over from this ignorant and dying élite? The country has gone through phases so distinctive that it is reasonable to make generalisations. Below them is a curious age-group of the people who were too young to catch the passion of the revolution; they were far less open to the fortifying faith of their immediate elders and spent the most formative period of their careers under full Stalinism from the later 1930s. Very many of this generation, now in their middle or late fifties, jump at shadows and cannot operate without instructions from above, however responsible their positions. The next age-group, now in its middle forties to early fifties, was abnormally small in number because of the effect of the First World War and the civil war on the birth-rate; and over 40 per cent of the men in this group were lost in the Second World War. The 'take-over generation' must include many of the people who are now in their late thirties and early forties, educated since the war, with far more technical expertise and sophistication than the generation of their parents and with plenty of self-confidence. It may soon be seen how this transition will affect, or is affecting, the pillars of Soviet society—the party apparat, the KGB, the officer corps, state administration, management, the professions and the arts.

6

Some Professions

People in particular occupations visiting Russia from the West readily understand their Soviet counterparts, if given the opportunity of free contact, but the understanding is within certain limits. The limits are imposed by differences in the nature of the societies. The following brief accounts of particular professions leave out features common to all countries and indicate those specific to the USSR.

STUDENTS

The world of most Soviet students is dominated, on the material side, by the problem of living on stipends of 25–35 rubles a month. It is almost impossible without help from parents. Opportunities to earn more exist, but are limited by the need to study up to 12 hours a day to do well, and the compulsory time spent on military training and harvesting. Unsatisfactory examination results may cause loss of the stipend for a semester, while consistent very high marks bring an increase of 25 per cent. Of the $1\frac{1}{2}$ million full-time students, the vast majority are in narrowly specialised technical and pedagogical institutes in the provincial towns. Hostel accommodation and canteens are similar to those for industrial workers and are cheap. About 30 per cent of the full-time students come from middle- or upper-class homes and receive no stipend. (In addition, about half a million study at evening courses and 1·7 million by correspondence.)

On the academic side, the dominating factor for the full-time students is usually the large number of lecture or laboratory hours, amounting to a normal working day, and insufficient time in the evening for both relaxation and memorising the book material. The courses are mostly four to five years, but tend to be overfilled with memory work. The amount to be learned is often recognised by the teaching staffs to be excessive; there is a consequent tendency to ease examinations, which are in any case oral wherever possible. Con-

Chemistry laboratory in a higher educational institution, Yerevan, Armenia

siderable reform is likely in teaching methods, which are now being called 'scholastic' in the press. In most of the 700 institutes and 40 universities the majority of students live in the hostels, where they are under surveillance by the KGB, which has offices in each institution, and more openly by the 'activists' of the Young Communist League, to which most students belong. In at least some institutions the league is now beginning to represent the interests of the students rather than those of the party and KGB.

For the majority of students, who will be technicians in industry, doctors and teachers, their pay is unlikely to be more than that of a skilled worker for many years after graduation or for their entire careers. They are, in principle, expected to take the opportunity of knowledge as its own reward. But higher education is nowadays the gateway to any career of consequence, in all fields, including business management and the party service. Since there is a strong desire for knowledge, and no recognised way to wealth other than in high state or party employment, there is very keen competition on both counts for places in higher education.

At the universities which enjoy most prestige there is some social bias in the selection of students. This is more marked in the arts and social sciences than in the natural sciences. Foreigners in the arts and social science section of Moscow University during the 1960s have met few, if any, Soviet students whose father is a rank-and-file industrial worker. Many of the staff in all kinds of higher educational institutions are not immune to social influence or even bribery. The son or daughter of a local political or industrial notable is distinctly less likely than others to fail the examination at the end of the probationary first year. Lecturers with the power to pass or fail students may be receiving money from their parents for private tuition on the tacit understanding that such tuition is effective. Students with access to foreign goods find little difficulty in getting special help from their tutors. As with selection of entrants, the tolerance of academic staffs to this kind of corruption is more widespread in the faculties where correct ideology is an important qualification.

As part of the 1958 educational reform, a two-year gap between leaving school and entering higher education was decreed, together with a good deal of work in production during the five years of study. In addition, local trade unions and party organisations were encouraged to select workers for higher education; these were officially allowed in without stringent entrance examinations. These methods of changing the social outlook and composition of students have proved unworkable. The 1964 and 1967 reforms restored, in principle, the former position by which the student body comes straight from school and concentrates upon study, apart from military training which amounts to four to six days a month for both sexes. However, when this training, the Marxism-Leninism courses and compulsory help by students in harvesting are taken into account, the normal five-year course amounts to four years or even three.

Students may be sent anywhere in the USSR for three years on graduation. This is a great help to the planners, who have to provide specialists for remote places, but the obligation is evaded by many graduates who, if their parents cannot pull strings, sometimes resort to desperate expedients. To get the planned number of new specialists where they are needed, the certificate of graduation is usually sent to the designated post, to be collected there by the graduate—in some cases one year after arrival; but this method is not always effective.

The planning of specialist labour has some effect on standards. Once a full-time student has passed the probationary year he is virtually bound to graduate. Any significant number of failures would mean underfulfilment of plan, both nationally and by the institution concerned. First degrees (which are called 'diplomas') are not divided into classes. The effect of examinations on stipends is, to some extent, an alternative incentive. Sometimes a failure is due to refusal to take or pass the examinations in the military training. This is extremely rare. More failures are caused by refusals to pass in Marxism-Leninism, but this is also rare. More important, perhaps, is refusal to take, or to pass in, the advanced Marxism-Leninism necessary for the first research degree (the 'Candidature,' equivalent in the non-ideological subjects to the British Ph.D.). One meets able young people in this dilemma, even though a 'candidate' is made for life and gets a middle-class salary as soon as he receives this qualification. Marriage, and in particular the birth of the first child, makes a big difference. The man gives way and accepts things as they are.

Full-time students have always been a special object of attention by the party officials responsible for explaining policy to the public. In 1965, after the fall of Khrushchev and the introduction of the economic reform, these officials became more flexible in meeting the critical outlook of students, especially in the more favoured central universities. Some reports of open discussions between the students at Moscow University and senior members of the Central Committee staff show little inhibition and fairly radical questions and comments. Other reports speak of unwillingness by students to give themselves away. Amongst the students themselves, orthodox views expressed in the language of *Pravda* are always sure of a hilarious response. The writer's experience of Soviet student mentality is summed up in what a physics undergraduate told him: 'They treat us as children and expect us to conquer space.'

JOURNALISTS

The great majority of Soviet newspapers and magazines, including those issued in large factories, belong to the party organisation of the area or factory in which they circulate. But the party also takes full responsibility for the remainder. Thus, at the top level, although *Izvestia* is the newspaper of the Supreme Soviet, in 1959 the Polit-bureau expressed dissatisfaction with this newspaper and instructed it to concentrate upon central and local administration, economic

V. Mayevsky, the political commentator of Pravda, *begins the day by reading the foreign press*

matters, ideology, science, culture, international affairs and Soviet foreign policy, and in 1960 transformed it from a morning to an evening newspaper. All journalists in controlling positions, such as editors, are on the appropriate party nomenklatura. The fact that many of their staffs are not party members makes no difference to the function of all journalists, without exception, as exponents and furtherers of the party's policies and views. It is, of course, impossible to run the vast number of central and local publications with the precision of a machine, but the department of the party headquarters which controls the press does its best, with the help of TASS (the government news agency) and the censorship, within the limits of human frailty and distance. Some of the problems of distance used to be overcome by TASS broadcasts, at dictation speed during the early afternoon and night, of principal news items for exact reproduction, and by flying out matrices of *Pravda*'s main pages from Moscow for local editions; but Soviet distances defeat even jet aircraft, and electronic means for more speedy reproduction are now being brought into use.

Central and republic newspapers are mostly a single sheet of four pages without advertisements, which costs two kopeks (a penny) and three kopeks when there is an extra two pages. Thus, despite the great circulation numbers, consumption of newsprint in the USSR is very low: about a twentieth of the United States. Important speeches and party statements, often very lengthy, are published in full locally as well as centrally: such an item may crowd almost everything else off the pages of the local papers for several days. The party's view of what is fit to print excludes crime, accidents, gossip, court reports, etc., except by political decision and in highly propagandist form as instances by which readers may be educated in civic virtue and the correct ideas. There is a strong Soviet tradition of voicing complaints by letters to the press, and of freelance local correspondents drawing attention to waste, inefficiency and injustice. The central press prints little of this, but has large staffs which investigate; the published results of such investigations are always within the same limits and purposes as everything else. The great bulk of the domestic material, local or national, is on production achievements.

Within these narrow limits, which are gradually and cautiously being broadened, newspaper journalists do a fairly good job. There is no lack of human interest and newsworthy happenings in Soviet life, including within the daily rounds of factories and farms; a little more of it gets into the newspapers, in a slightly less didactic form, and the photographs become less austere, as the years go by. Elements of weekend magazine reading are beginning to appear in some of the central newspapers. But at its present rate of progress the Soviet press will not become a reliable reflection of life for several generations yet. Soviet people, including journalists, find it difficult to understand why foreign students of their country read their newspapers. This task is indeed unattractive because of the patently insincere and even hysterical reporting and the murderous monotony of the ideological articles, but it is unavoidable in building up a picture of the country. (Readers of this book who wish to see for themselves are advised to look at any issue of the weekly *Current Digest of the Soviet Press*, which conveniently brings together in English translation only the most interesting items and excerpts, from a wide range of Russian newspapers, weekly magazines and monthly journals. The same is done, more briefly, in the supplement to the quarterly *Soviet Studies*.)

The central daily Russian newspapers are: *Pravda* (Truth), the organ of the Politbureau, which sets the political tone every day (it appears seven days of the week); the government newspaper *Izvestia* (News) and its weekly illustrated supplement; *Komsomolskaya Pravda*, owned by the Young Communist League; *Trud* (Labour), owned by the Central Council of Trade Unions; *Krasnaya Zvezda* (Red Star), organ of the Ministry of Defence, and an agricultural and a railway newspaper. The other central newspapers appear two or three times a week and are owned by the appropriate ministry or trade union or both jointly; they include those for the timber industry, water transport, construction, cultural workers, teachers, the medical professions and athletics.

The writers' weekly, *Literaturnaya Gazeta*, has a tradition of liveliness on general topics and safe conformity on literature. There are few other weeklies, the outstanding one being *Ekonomicheskaya Gazeta*, which publishes excellent informative discussions on industry at the factory and planning levels: it is owned by the party and is permitted a special frankness, of which its staff make admirable use, as a forum for the acute problem of industrial organisation. The humorous magazine *Krokidil*, which appears every 10 days in a circulation of nearly five million, is capable of brilliantly satirical drawings, but the brilliance is in sad contrast with the narrow range of topics and the low levels of officialdom which it is licensed to satirise. The two illustrated monthly magazines for women—*Woman Worker* (10 million circulation) and *Peasant Woman* (5·7 million)— are mainly about work, elementary politics and domestic matters, including clothes. They have improving stories, a few advertisements, and contain garment-patterns which look very complicated, all the shapes being overprinted on each other. One of the monthly journals specialises on fashions and several others include such items.

The numerous other central monthly publications fall into several groups. About a dozen are mainly literary, publishing short stories, poetry, criticism, new novels in instalments before book publication, and sophisticated articles of general interest. They each have a distinct editorial character and fairly large circulations; some are relatively liberal and are liable to have their paper ration reduced if they overstep the mark. However, by 1968 it was becoming possible in the best of the literary monthlies to say anything about any subject —not outright, but by historical analogy and in other Aesopian forms. Teachers have about 20 monthlies, mostly on particular subjects in the syllabus. There are many scholarly monthly journals in ideologically sensitive fields such as history, economics and philosophy, in which serious and pseudo scholarship are curiously

The public procurator addresses the court

mixed. Their editors tread a sometimes exciting tight-rope between the needs of research and what is politically possible. More truly journalistic are the mass-circulation monthlies for particular audiences and purposes, such as science and technology for young people, which can be very good. Specialist journals of technology and the natural sciences do not now differ in any significant way from their counterparts in other countries.

In addition to the Russian press, the same kind of newspapers and magazines are published in 58 other languages of the USSR.

LAWYERS

A Soviet citizen going to law applies to the Collegium of Advocates in his town. Advocates combine the work of solicitors and barristers. They operate only as members of their local collegium, which shares out the work amongst them and takes the fees, paying about 75 per cent back to the member and keeping the remainder for social insurance and holiday pay of members and the expenses of the collegium. The maximum earnings of advocates and of collegium employees were laid down in 1965 by the government of the Latvian republic for the main collegium of the capital city, Riga: advocates—150 rubles per month (with certain deductions); salary of the elected president of the collegium—240 rubles (plus not more than 60 rubles from his fees); wages of collegium employees—40–45 rubles for cleaners and messengers; 50–60 rubles for typists; 70–115 rubles for bookkeepers and auditors. A member of the Riga collegium told the author that this decree had been keenly resented as the only instance of an upper limit imposed on earnings in a free profession. Consequently, the Latvian government had unofficially allowed the ceiling to be about twice the 150 rubles in the decree. No other Soviet republic had imposed an earnings ceiling on its lawyers.

Maximum charges in Riga were fixed in great detail in the same decree, as follows. Legal advice is free to anybody if the advocate does not need to study documents, and not more than two rubles if he does. Suits for alimony and for industrial disease or injury benefit are free at all stages, but not for the defender. Suits between collective farms and their members are free to both parties. In civil cases, fees for preparing documents are two to six rubles; for putting a client's case to an official—six rubles; for representing clients in court—six rubles per day; for preparing an appeal—five rubles; for work in a rehearing—50 per cent of the fees for the original case. Fees in criminal cases are higher, up to 40 rubles for the first day's work in court on an exceptionally involved case. It is well known that a competent advocate makes much more than 150 rubles a month and a brilliant one immensely more, and that they keep the illegally high fees for themselves, just as renowned tailors earn far more than they are supposed to as members of a tailoring workshop. The wealthiest Soviet lawyers are said to be those who specialise most successfully in the legal intricacies of large-scale and high-level economic crime. There is reluctance amongst law students to become advocates, whose social status is not high. In part, this is because a client's interests can be honestly represented in court only if the issues involved are a matter of indifference to the current party policy and the local officials.

The People's Courts (local courts of first instance) must act as educative institutions. The judge, who is usually legally trained, is paid 150 rubles a month and is in form elected for five years by the citizens of the locality. He sits with two lay assessors who are also locally elected; they usually display little initiative in the proceedings but retire with the judge to reach the decision. There is no jury system. Where no lesson for the public is deemed to be involved, cases may be fought hard and with skill by the advocates on both sides. Decisions may be appealed, or their revision requested, by interested parties or the local procurator. The Procurator-General of the USSR is the chief legal officer of the state: his local representatives prosecute in criminal cases and have the duty of checking that proper legal procedure is observed by the courts (and by all state organisations), but like advocates and judges they work entirely within the requirements of party policy. Criminal trials are prepared for hearing, as in several continental countries, by a pre-trial procedure which goes into all relevant matters. Soviet pre-trial procedure is in effect the occasion for deciding the course and results of criminal cases. Criminal trials are thus frequently educative show trials, held in a local theatre or meeting-hall.

It has recently become possible to bring actions against state institutions and to sue newspapers for libel. But few people in the USSR are likely to have any confidence in the law if the party's interpretation of the public interest is involved in their case. Some legal theorists have for many years courageously argued in favour of the rule of law, not as a general principle, for that would be anti-party, but on limited points of legislation, insofar as the editors of their learned journals find such arguments possible to print. However, the general public in Russia appears to have little interest in this idea. What the public wants is justice, not law. The feeling that justice can be somehow obtained without much bother about respect for law is deep-rooted and still very strong amongst Russians. But they are learning the hard way—as all the democratic countries have done. Young people are beginning to raise basic questions about infringements of the constitution by the party authorities. The constitution is a fine-sounding document introduced by Stalin in December 1936, when the great purge was well under way. It out-does all democratic constitutions in guaranteeing the rights of citizens, but it is unlikely that anybody has taken this seriously. Now, however, people in the younger generation are not only putting the question: 'What right has the party to override the law?', but are doing so in the form of defending the constitutional principle.

The party officially recognises the need to replace the Stalin constitution, and for about 10 years a special commission, which sat under the chairmanship of Khrushchev until his fall, has been trying to draft a new one. Nothing seems to have come of it. The present period, which is one of striking contradiction between society's need

for the orderliness of law and the apparat's inability to allow itself to
be trammelled by law, is not the best time in which to introduce a
new constitution. The commission is said to have abandoned its
labours in 1968.

There is a special branch of Soviet law which handles about a
million cases a year, called 'state arbitration.' Since nearly all business
enterprises are parts of the single state, they cannot sue each other
for failure to observe contracts. In any case, they are told what
contracts to make with each other, within the plans of supply and
delivery prepared by the industrial ministries and the state planning
committee. Disputes about contracts between state enterprises are
heard and settled by the arbitration courts. If two factories cannot
agree on the details of the contract, the case goes to such a court,
which decides the details and the contract is then binding. If the
contract is broken (which in many, if not most, cases is due to a
factory's plan being changed by its ministry), they again go to an
arbitration court, which decides who is in the right and how restitu-
tion is to be made. These courts employ a combination of legal,
industrial and financial expertise. Their staffs are particularly aware
of the urgent need for sanctity of contract; much of their work lies in
coping with the disruptive effects of high bureaucratic and party
decisions. (Contract cases where a citizen or a non-state institution is
in dispute with a state institution are decided in the ordinary courts.)

Since the revolution the party leaders have had an ambivalent
attitude to the training of lawyers and the work of legal theorists. For
the first 15 years law was regarded as something destined to dis-
appear, although for the time being Soviet law codes had to be drawn
up and statutes drafted. Then, from the middle 1930s, law was
officially regarded as a necessary instrument for a long time to come
in the defence of the regime against any conceivable threat, but this
function of law was not to be weakened by any niceties of its interpretation or operation. After Stalin, law as a profession became rather
more acceptable to the party leaders, but not entirely so. It was one
of the subjects in which full-time courses were in part abolished by
Khrushchev, who appears to have thought that training in evening
and correspondence courses should suffice. The subject is now again
taught full-time. Party opinion as to the function of lawyers under the
harmonious social relations of Full Communism is not clear. Mean-
while, law graduates prefer a career in state arbitration, the procuracy,
and as lawyers attached to state enterprises, rather than as advocates
or judges.

TEACHERS

A teacher now approaching retiring age has seen the creation of the profession in its present size and form. Primary schooling was becoming universal when the war caused a great setback. Since then full secondary education (the '10-year school', beginning at the age of seven) has expanded sufficiently for it to become compulsory, according to the government's present intention, by 1970. The very quick growth of the profession was made possible by recruiting women, who

The 'repeater' pupil. 'Why, that's Tanya! We sat at the same desk in the first form'

now form 80 per cent of the teachers (but less than a quarter of school heads), and by standardising the curriculum, textbooks, syllabuses and even lesson-content throughout the country, with heavy emphasis on memorising and learning by rote. The extreme standardisation probably made the work of a large proportion of the quickly trained teachers more effective but, now that the profession is maturing, uniformity is proving irksome and is less necessary. The new developments announced in 1967–8 are: a higher proportion of men teachers; emphasis on 'learning by discovery' (which must entail great changes in teacher-training); more variety within the standard curriculum; and more schools. The last improvement is urgent, as a third of the schools now teach in two shifts, some in three and some—at least until the early 1960s—even in four. A recent pay increase brought the great majority of teachers into a range of 70–120 rubles a month.

Our retiring teacher has experienced rather drastic and sudden changes in policy. Coeducation, which had been universal, was abolished during the war and was again made universal in the mid-1950s before the organisational upheaval of its abolition was over. An educational reform in 1958 introduced vocational training, rising to a third of the time in the upper forms. In August 1964, less than three weeks before the new school year began on 1 September, vocational training was reduced without prior warning and the year that had been added to the full secondary curriculum in 1958 was taken off again, which meant that pupils entering the abolished eleventh form and those entering the tenth had to take their subsequent leaving examinations together. The situation was so confused that the Minister of Education of the Russian republic, which has about a million teachers, announced in the press that anybody in doubt as to what to do should telephone him personally. A few years earlier, the social studies course was introduced so suddenly, in the middle of the 1962/3 session, that it had to be taught from chapters serialised in the teachers' newspaper. The key concept of this course —that the pupils would live under Full Communism—had to be removed and forgotten a few years later. In the non-Russian schools the amount of time devoted to Russian language and literature has fluctuated, sometimes sharply, and in some republics even the alphabet changed twice before the war (from the Arabic to the Latin and from that to the Slavonic).

Secondary-school teachers are trained in five-year institutes from the age of 17–18. Primary teachers are mostly trained in four-year colleges from the age of 15. The work of teachers and schools is evaluated to a large extent on the proportion of pupils who fail the end-of-year examinations and have to stay in the same form. Education is compulsory until completion of the eighth form, so repeaters may be kept at school for one or several years over the age of 15, but ways are found of letting them go. There is a statistical average of about 20 pupils per teacher, but the average size of classes is substantially larger. In the one-shift schools lessons start early, are completed by a late lunch break and children return in the afternoons for homework and pastimes. The practice of 'prolonged-day' schooling, whereby children spend up to 12 hours in the school, is increasing, mainly as a convenience for working mothers and in areas of bad home conditions. Headmasters find it difficult to avoid bringing pressure on the teachers' own time (especially for supervision in prolonged-day schools), on which heavy inroads are made, in any case, by numerous meetings for political and organisational purposes.

The boarding schools, which were until recently intended to include all children in due course, have proved to be too expensive. The prolonged day is a cheaper alternative means of supervised upbringing. An extensive system of apprenticeship schools is operated in association with industry for those leaving school at 15, and this may be brought within the secondary school system to facilitate compulsory 10-year schooling by 1970.

There is supposed to be no separation of bright and dull children apart from special schools for the handicapped. Such separation exists in practice, to varying extents in different towns. Where there is a strong demand for juvenile labour and the local authorities are prepared to overlook the law, it is not difficult for children whose parents so wish to leave before 15. Where the demand to stay on after 15 exceeds places available the headmaster sits on a selection committee with representatives of the local educational, political and industrial authorities, who use as criteria the teachers' recommendations and the family background. Differences of repute and staff morale have emerged between even neighbouring schools: the headmaster of a good one finds means of transferring undesired pupils to a weaker school, despite the catchment-area regulations.

The really good out-of-school facilities, such as 'pioneer palaces' in the large towns, which can provide for only a very small proportion of schoolchildren, tend to be monopolised by the best pupils as a reward for good work and by children of the best families, which accentuates differences in attainment. The schools of special opportunity, such as those which teach in foreign languages or take mathematically gifted children, have been too few to affect the general picture. Their number is now increasing fairly rapidly and parents' pressure for places in them is becoming a social issue. Inequalities of opportunity are due, above all, to better schooling in the big towns than in the villages and small towns, and to differences in home conditions and cultural background. The authorities make big efforts to overcome the results of past and present inequality by providing evening schools for young workers and adults who wish to complete a primary or secondary education (there are five million such pupils at present), and by correspondence courses on a very large scale in secondary, junior technical and higher education, with paid holidays for pre-examination study. But the low effectiveness of such 'second-chance' facilities in relation to their cost is now being pointed out in the press. These facilities certainly give school-teachers opportunity for extra earnings.

The amount of education declines steeply with increasing age in the working class. Sample surveys indicate that perhaps a third of industrial workers over the age of 30 in the provincial factory towns have had not more than four years of schooling, while a high proportion of their children have, or will soon have, 10 years. In 1950 the number of pupils completing the full secondary course was about equal to the number of places available in higher education, whereas at present there are no places for three out of four of those who complete secondary school and wish to enter higher education. The number of young people who cannot get a place as a student but do not want to stay in the working class constitutes a serious social problem, which the 1958 educational reform tried to meet and failed.

The world of Soviet teachers and pupils leaves conflicting impressions on the observer: an intense desire to give and to get knowledge; the monotony of the highly standardised lessons, ideological blinkers and learning by rote; the low social status of teachers and their difficulties in imposing discipline; the disruptive effects of sudden or insufficiently prepared decisions by the Politbureau and their too hasty implementation; the excessive demands of homework on pupils and of meetings on teachers; the effectiveness of parent-teacher contact where this is systematically developed; the great effort by the state to provide educational equality and the powerful social tendencies in the opposite direction. There is no lack of desire amongst teachers to help produce good citizens, but not all of them enjoy the elaborate organising of the Young Pioneer detachments to

An operation to restore the hearing of an otosclerosis patient

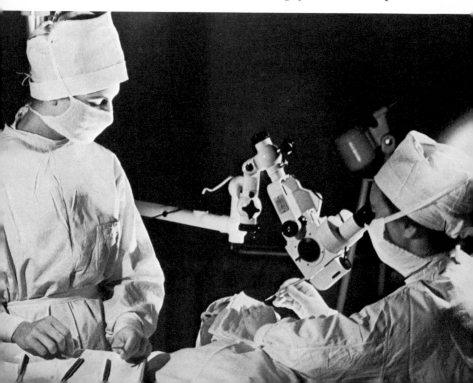

which all the younger children from the age of nine belong, or working with the Young Communist League which embraces the older pupils, or having to destroy religious ideas, which children continue to get from their mothers or grandmothers.

At a Moscow secondary school in April 1968 a staff meeting was convened by the teachers' trade union, on the instructions of the party committee, to recommend the dismissal of one of their number for political unreliability. This teacher was one of 220 signatories to a letter of protest against the illegal procedure at a trial of young writers. The accused teacher defended her action on the grounds that a struggle for observance of the law was essential to avoid a relapse into Stalinism. The five teachers who voted against her dismissal were themselves threatened with dismissal by the headmaster. The discussion showed resentment by several teachers at her practice of telling the pupils about poets of the early Soviet period whose names they were not supposed to know. These teachers had been embarrassed by awkward questions at literature and history lessons. Of the 37 teachers who voted for dismissal, some who spoke showed a complete inability to understand why legal procedures should be observed when dealing with 'enemies'. The teacher was dismissed but later reinstated.

DOCTORS

Medical schools are beginning to show a preference for men and the very high proportion of women doctors is already declining. There are extraordinary differences in the doctor-patient ratio between small towns and large, backward and advanced regions, country and town; and above all between the social classes and occupations in the towns because of the special services for a great variety of privileged groups. But these differences are gradually being reduced. There are more doctors in proportion to the total population than in the Western countries. The standard of training is not high and the pharmaceutical industry is considered by some specialists to be about 15 years behind that of the West. Medical students are told that tuberculosis and syphilis have been eliminated in the USSR, then find these diseases rife when posted to backward areas. A fully qualified woman doctor starts at about 70 rubles a month. A male provincial general practitioner with several years' experience is paid 110–120 rubles and gets what extra he can by private treatment. Patients most in need of it cannot afford to pay him and their illness is often connected with inadequate diet. There are acute local shortages even of aspirin. Experienced doctors tend to occupy a special place in

present-day provincial society: they can communicate with the different generations, who cannot understand each other, and they find that patients use them almost as confessors. With luck, personality and a certain hardness, a male provincial general practitioner can live fairly well, with a car and a boat. Traditional medical ethics have been excluded from medical training for nearly 50 years, being replaced by duty to the state, but something like it is now coming back. However, respect for the confidences of patients is not likely to be permitted. The ambulance service is crippled, outside the big cities and the Baltic republics, by lack of surfaced local roads.

A book-stall in Moscow, run by the state-owned book trade

PUBLISHING

Like newspapers and magazines, publishing houses are owned by a variety of organisations. Their two main problems, apart from censorship—which is so much part of the business that it is taken for granted—are paper and finance. There is always a shortage of paper, and each group of publishers fights hard for its share in the annual allocation by the State Planning Committee to the Press Council (a government body which controls all publishing and coordinates the plans of all publishers). As for finance, publishers are, like other firms, expected to make a profit, but at the same time they have to issue books, often in very large editions, which are regarded as politically desirable but do not enjoy much demand. Such books can be seen on the shelves of libraries in many copies, untouched, since it is the duty of librarians to acquire them and this provides at least a basic market.

Yet texts of new laws are sometimes chained to the wall in libraries because so few copies are published. Publishers are always on the lookout for ideologically flawless works which will also sell. Hence the occasional publication in large editions of sadistic and erotic historical thrillers on themes of good Reds versus bad Whites. The Sherlock Holmes stories, which are considered ideologically harmless although foreign, sell in enormous numbers, as they did before the revolution. The economic reform, which by 1968 was reaching the publishing houses, is said to have encouraged some of them to take more chances with the censorship, in poetry especially, because of the official emphasis on making a good profit.

Many books are published for limited circulation: students specialising in philosophy, for example, study Bertrand Russell's *History of Western Philosophy* and the history of Russian philosophy by Zenkovsky (an émigré theologian), appropriately edited, but

Poetry Day: Yevtushenko giving autographs to readers

unknown to the bookshops. In 1937 the Webbs' *Soviet Communism; a New Civilisation* was beautifully translated and printed in Moscow in 10,000 copies, but the bookshops there had not heard of it. There was interest in this book at the time amongst the political élite and the translation was probably made to satisfy their curiosity by confidential distribution, as was a translation of Churchill's war memoirs more recently. One of the curiosities of Soviet publishing in recent years is the Russian translations of foreign literary works whose authors, quite unknown in their own countries, specialise in writing suitable 'foreign' novels for the Soviet market.

WRITERS

The Union of Soviet Writers has about 6,500 members. With very few exceptions, nobody else is recognised as a professional author. The union has very large sums available in its 'Litfund', mainly from a percentage on book sales and theatre takings, out of which it subsidises authors in many ways, helps potential members and runs an Institute of Literature. This institute trains writers of literature in a four-year course, with the possibility of another three years as postgraduates; there is also a special two-year 'improvement' course for members of the union. The institute had in 1967 students from 49 nations, large and small, of the USSR. The union itself, established in 1932 as the sole and compulsory organisation for literature, was directed for many years by Alexander Fadeyev, a novelist of considerable talent and personality who subordinated his literary strength to party loyalty, kept the writers in order, and shot himself when Stalin was denounced in 1956. Occasional rebellions against party control break out in local branches, but soon subside.

The union requires all members to subscribe to the principles of socialist realism, which enjoins 'a truthful, historically concrete representation of reality in its revolutionary development'. In practice, this amounts to a kind of statuesque hypocrisy which takes the party's ideal of 'Soviet man' as more real than actual life and places on writers the duty of influencing their readers in the direction of the ideal. This canon of literature is ceasing to be enforceable in its original crudity, though it is only very rarely evaded altogether. Entire areas of life and art remain out of bounds. Membership of the union involves frequent organisational meetings, and discussions of other members' work in progress—both as helpful criticism and as an additional stage of censorship. The great majority of members are hacks making good money; many are gifted men with broken souls;

some skilfully enlarge the area of honesty, but their honesty becomes sly in the process. Much is written 'for the drawer' without hope of foreseeable publication, both by members of the union and by others who despise it.

There are standard rates. Prose is paid at 200–400 rubles for 40,000 ems (about 24 foolscap pages of double-spaced typescript), depending on the author's standing, and at decreasing rates for subsequent editions (e.g. 50 per cent for a fifth edition). For purposes of payment an 'edition' is taken as 15,000 copies for prose and 5,000 for poetry; actual editions are usually a good deal larger. It is possible for a moderately successful author to make a very good income, and for those most widely published to make fortunes, but special rates for 'mass publication' books now impose limits on the highest earnings.

There is increasing evidence of a great literature struggling to emerge, arising from the need to state openly and explore freely the range of human experience in Russia over the past 50 years. Free Soviet writings published abroad are beginning to constitute a branch of contemporary world literature. Some of the disobedient writers who have in recent years been placed in mental hospitals are indeed unbalanced. To live in the world of Soviet art without losing touch with one's artistic conscience invites a kind of schizophrenia. An informed study of contemporary Soviet literature would note the various ways in which the stronger spirits cope with this situation.

At the second congress of Soviet writers, held in 1954, the then Minister of Culture noted the high cost of mistakes in censorship. An incorrect novel, he declared, carries error into every corner of the country and into millions of minds, which requires the labour of thousands of party and state officials to cure. This remains the official view—which is now so much out of touch with the temper of a large section of educated opinion that there is a feeling that anything may happen. The outstanding case of suppression during 1968 concerns the novels and plays of Alexander Solzhenitsyn, one of the world's great writers, who had asked the Union of Soviet Writers to protect him, as a member, from persecution by the political police. His works circulate very widely but illegally in Russia. Those available have been published abroad.

SOCIOLOGISTS

Sociology is the study of the parts of society, whether entire classes or small groups, in their relations with each other and with society as a whole. Sociologists gather data on the structure of society, on factors which affect it such as educational and economic opportunity and public opinion, on particular social problems such as crime and racial relations, on suicide and other ways in which people opt out. Sociology was in effect banned in the USSR not long after the revolution because free enquiry in its field challenged the official theories and policies. Now that the administration of the country urgently needs sociological information and analyses, the subject has reappeared, but in a restricted way. The party bureaus at various levels have established 'tame' amateur research groups whose function is to gather information on such problems as why so many workers change their jobs frequently or impair their efficiency by drink. But any such information which may embarrass the official ideology is not published. The bureau of a large industrial town may be responsible for 100,000 party members and need sample surveys, of a more or less sociological kind, to be made of them.

At the same time, sociology has reappeared as an academic discipline, usually within the philosophy departments of universities. The academic sociologists, in addition to conducting important 'concrete' investigations for the government, are beginning to enquire into forbidden matters, such as the class structure of Soviet society. Amongst themselves natural scientists as well as sociologists discuss, for example, cybernetic theories of society which point to the need for feed-back between government and the governed, for which democracy is necessary. The present situation in academic sociology is that the political authorities make use of it but have not permitted the establishment of a sociological journal or any academic department of sociology or a genuine association of sociologists; the subject is not taught as such and no textbook on it has been published. Soviet sociologists study the techniques of their subject from a limited range of foreign publications or from typewritten translations of the more valuable foreign articles and books which circulate amongst them. Some have managed to build up excellent personal libraries of foreign sociological works. In particular, they have contact with Polish, Czech and Hungarian sociologists whose governments permit far more freedom of investigation and who work on problems which are similar in certain respects to Soviet social problems.

It is most unlikely that a social science so necessary for effective administration can be kept for long in this condition. It is also impossible for this science, insofar as it becomes free to investigate and publish, to avoid building up a picture of Soviet society and its problems which differs greatly from that presented in the official set of ideas. Sociology as a science is attracting able young people in the USSR, despite the difficulties in gathering data and the other limitations noted above.

PRIESTS

Russia may have a higher proportion of regular church attenders than many other industrial countries. The number for the Orthodox Church is usually estimated at 30 million or more. Of the other large religion, Islam, most of the 25 million population in the Moslem republics are said to be believers. There is, however, no

The last remaining synagogue in Moscow

clear line between religion and national sentiment in Islam. This is also true, to some extent, of Russian Orthodox Christians. Despite the great efforts put into propagating atheism over the past 50 years, backed by the power of the state, few people are active atheists by conviction and there is probably less of the passive kind than in Western populations. Amongst educated people, where passive atheism is most widespread, there have been signs of increased interest in religion during the 1960s, at the same time as the official campaign against religion has been intensified. In this campaign, since 1961 half of the 20,000 Orthodox churches then in use have been closed and many priests, who find special difficulty in getting other work, have been sacked. The method of closing churches has been to use a decree of 1961 which established parish councils of 20 persons as the authority over the church, with the priest as their employee who has no other legal function than to conduct church services. It has been difficult for priests to refuse their normal functions in births, marriages and deaths, but to perform them may be a sufficient reason for dismissal and closure of the church. Even to explain to parishioners that it has

СОДЕРЖАТЕЛЬНИЦА ПРИТОНА

A hand-drawn poster of a named local religious woman, who is depicted as keeping a brothel

become illegal has been considered an offence in some places. Penetration of or influence upon the Councils of Twenty by the local party organisation has resulted in the wholesale dismissal of priests and closure of churches 'at the request of the believers themselves'. These measures may have considerably reduced the number of churchgoers noted at the beginning of this paragraph.

In the Moslem areas, which depend less on clergy, the effect of the anti-priest campaign is less. Some Catholic areas were acquired after the war and, so far as is known, remain stoutly Catholic; but in the postwar territories the Uniate Church—that part of the Orthodox religion which accepts the Pope—was extirpated by the combined efforts of the political police and the Orthodox Church. Judaism has been harried with special energy and scarcely any synagogues or rabbis remain, while a striking recrudescence of the Jewish national identity has reappeared amongst young people. The 'Old Believers' of the Russian Church now number only about a million and apparently stand firm in the few areas where they live. The Baptist and associated groups, which amount to a Protestant development within the Russian religious outlook, appear to be increasing amongst the provincial working class, and are specially suspect as un-Russian. Of the 16,000 lamas in the main Buddhist area in Eastern Siberia, 300 remain.

The leaders of the religious communities (except the Jews, who are not recognised as a community) have more or less formal relations with the Soviet government, which permits a very small number of seminaries for training priests and ministers. The Baptist leaders are regarded by part of their flock as both too narrow theologically and too willing to compromise; the consequent breakaway movement is severely persecuted by the state. Tendencies towards a similar split are becoming visible in the Orthodox Church where many of the higher clergy have long made their peace with the state. Many people in the USSR believe that the party is trying to abolish religion in time for Full Communism by compromising the leaders, eliminating the priests and closing the churches.

Foreign specialists on Soviet law find an extraordinary confusion, looseness of wording and obscurity in the laws concerning religion. Soviet citizens who need to know what is permitted in religious activities and what may be criminal or civil offences cannot obtain such information or work it out for themselves from the published enactments with any certainty. This can only be deliberate policy on the part of the authorities. The general standard of Soviet law as regards consistency and accessibility is poor. But in the religious field it is absurdly so. Law is thus used in a special sense against religion. In practice, to some extent a locality has its own changeable and arbitrary rules, depending on instructions given by the local representative of the government's Council for the Affairs of Religious Cults. These officials are quite liable to countermand known laws, but only by word of mouth, not in writing; nevertheless, their decisions have to be obeyed.

Palace of Weddings, Kiev

The government of the Russian republic recently set up a committee for devising and introducing into daily life new secular ceremonies and rituals. The first 'Palace of Weddings' had been established about 1960 to provide a non-religious ceremonial and a setting more attractive than a dingy registry office. There are secular rituals for christenings, burial services, golden weddings, receiving the passport at the age of 16, vows on entering particular trades and the vow taken at school by all children on joining the Young Pioneers. As a secular use of the tradition of saints' days there are special days for the army, air force, artillery, tank troops, miners, teachers, railwaymen, iron and steel workers, builders, fishermen, oil and gas workers and many others. Campaigns to promote such observances and introduce new ones usually coincide with party instructions to accentuate anti-religious activity. One such confidential instruction, in 1963, noted that 40 per cent of all marriages in the Moscow area were still being solemnised in church. (A year earlier, the writer was told by the manager of the Palace of Weddings in Leningrad that marriage in church had virtually ceased there since his institution had opened.) The party's efforts to meet needs traditionally met by religion seem to focus increasingly on the person of Lenin, who is presented as in some sense eternal. Banners proclaim: 'Lenin lived, Lenin lives, Lenin will live.'

Russia in 1968 gives an impression of a tension that the writer has not observed there before. Social emotions of great force and complexity have been evident enough in previous experience of the country. The charged atmosphere of the present time carries a sense of some necessary or impending resolution of feelings and thoughts. The Russian nation may need all its great spiritual resources to manage whatever adjustment it faces. It will need its genius for the combination of colour, sound and community expressed in its church services. Lenin-worship, Full Communism, parades and miners days are not yet an adequate substitute.

Postscript

Many parts of the Soviet scene have been omitted from this book, for example the different ways of life of different nations within the single political and economic framework, life in the armed forces, the world of small children and that of adolescents. The most important aspect that has been left out is happiness. People make the best of their circumstances anywhere. They get what satisfactions and enjoyments may be going. And they cope with their own governments and bureaucracies more readily than foreigners may find credible. They know the short cuts. Plenty of happiness is to be found in Russia. Watching the thousands of young people going out skiing on a Sunday morning, picking mushrooms with a family party in the woods, catching the excitement of some assistants in a bookshop discussing the relative merits of two different productions of a new play, or of parents about their new baby, one feels that a suspicious, strident and interfering government does not loom so large after all. In any case, there is deep satisfaction in the sense of community, the feel of a whole nation as a kind of large family, which remains fairly strong in Russia. The Soviet system itself is in some way an outcome of the Russians' reluctance to lose this sense of community as they came into the modern world during the past three or four generations.

But while one must bring in simple happiness to keep the record straight, the preceding paragraph is not true as it stands. The system cannot really be escaped. The young skiers are old enough to have mastered something of the finesse of the Soviet double life. Not only the parents but the children in the family party may be considering as they picnic in the woods whether certain neighbours know that they are spending the day with a foreigner. The girls in the bookshop have not seen both productions, for tickets are hard to come by and expensive; the play itself (*Irkutsk Story*) has the special falsity of late socialist realism; and excitement about such things is the product of a certain narrowness of life. Finally, whatever success the Russians may have achieved in their great effort to avoid the loneliness and aimlessness of Western individualism, their Marxism-Leninism is at least as conventional as religion is in the West, and their informer system makes for a special isolation of people from each other.

Appendix

SOME SOVIET PRICES IN MID-1968 AND THEIR
  BRITISH EQUIVALENTS

The difficulties in equating prices in the two countries are very great. For example, the quality of most clothing, some foods such as meat, and services such as rush-hour transport, is lower than what is normally available in Britain.

Item	*Price*	*Price in Britain*	*Value of the Ruble*
Food			
Bread—rye	14–18*k.* per kilo	No equivalent	—
Bread—wheat	30*k.* per kilo	1*s.* 6*d.* per 1¾ lb. loaf	6*s.* 4*d.*
Three-course meal in canteen-type eating-place	80*k.*	5*s.*	6*s.* 3*d.*
Meat in state shops	(various kinds, averaged)	3*s.*	
Sugar, granulated	1*r.* 4*k.* per kilo	9*d* per lb.	1*s.* 8*d.*
Tea	48*k.* per 50 grams	2*s.* per ¼ lb.	1*s.* 10*d.*
Butter	3*r.* 60*k.* per kilo	3*s.* 6*d.* per lb.	2*s.* 2*d.*
Clothing			
Man's suit	150*r.*	£13	1*s.* 9*d.*
Woman's suit	102*r.*	£6	1*s.* 3*d.*
Wool pullover or jumper	40*r.*	£2	1*s.*
Cotton summer dress	7*r.*	£1 5*s.*	3*s.* 6*d.*
Leather shoes	50*r.*	£3	1*s.* 3*d.*
Housing, Travel and Education			
Standard rent, per month, state housing	15*k.*–32*k.* per sq. metre	Say 5*s.* per sq. metre (council housing at £3 per week)	16*s.*–33*s.*
Bus, tram or tube fare	3–5*k.* per journey, any distance	Say 10*d.* per journey	£1
98 octane petrol	10*k.* per litre	6*s.* per gallon	13*s.* 4*d.*
Paper-backed book	30*k.*	3*s.* 6*d.*	12*s.*
Slide rule	2*r.* 7*k.*	25*s.*	12*s.*
Drink and Tobacco	(averaged)		10*s.*

What the Soviet citizen buys from the state may roughly be classified in five groups: cheap food (bread and grain products, canteen-type meals, drink); dear foods (almost all others); cheap non-foods (cultural goods, tobacco); dear non-foods (mainly clothing); services (housing and urban fares are cheap, inter-city fares and entertainments dearer). From official Soviet trade statistics and some guesswork, the following composition of each 100 rubles spent by the public on state goods and services may be supposed:

Cheap food	20r. worth 6s. per ruble	= £6 0s.
Dear food	32r. worth 2s. per ruble	= £3 4s.
Cheap non-food	6r. worth 12s. per ruble	= £3 12s.
Dear non-food	30r. worth 1s. 6d. per ruble	= £2 5s.
Services	12r. worth 15s. per ruble	= £9 0s.
	100r.	£24 1s.

On this basis, a ruble is worth just under 5s.—as an average for all sections of the population in what they buy from the state. If differences of quality are taken fully into account for all items, the ruble would be worth rather less. While this book was in the press a specialist study appeared: Philip Hanson, *The Consumer in the Soviet Economy*, London, Macmillan, 1968. From Mr. Hanson's data and calculations a value of 6s.–7s. for the ruble in 1964–65 may be inferred (and a higher value in 1968, since prices have risen faster in Britain than in Russia). If Mr. Hanson is correct, the value of Soviet wages in British money given in this book should be increased by about 50%. However, the writer considers his own estimate of 4s.–5s. in 1968 to be more realistic.

Select Bibliography

PUBLICATIONS MENTIONED IN THE TEXT

Nikolai Ostrovsky, *How the Steel was Tempered*, 2 vols., Moscow, Foreign Languages Publishing House (no date). (Also published as: Nicholas Ostrovski, *The Making of a Hero*, International Publishers, New York, 1937)

A. S. Yesenin-Volpin, *Vesennii list/A Leaf of Spring* (Russian text, with English translation by George Reavey), London, 1961

Y. Daniel, *This is Moscow Speaking*, London, Harvill Press, 1964

Abram Tertz (Sinyavsky), *The Trial Begins* (1960); *The Icicle* (1963); *The Makepeace Experiment* (1965), London, Collins/Harvill

A. Solzhenitsyn, *The First Circle* and *The Cancer Ward* (parts I and II), London, 1968

Georgi Shakhnazarov (ed.), *Man, Science and Society*, Moscow, Progress Publishers, 1965. This is the first English publication of the Social Studies textbook summarised in chapter 1. It may have been in process of translation when Khrushchev was removed from the party leadership; the quotations from his speeches, together with the promise of Full Communism by 1980 and the figures of the long-term production plans for 1970 and 1980, have been omitted. Otherwise this translation, which became available in 1968, is virtually the same as the 1964 Russian edition

The Current Digest of the Soviet Press (weekly), edited by Leo Gruliow, 351 Riverside Drive, New York, New York 10025, USA. (Very expensive, but worth recommending to large public libraries)

Information Supplement (quarterly), obtainable from Soviet Studies, University of Glasgow (10s. per year)

Programme of the Communist Party of the Soviet Union, Moscow, Foreign Languages Publishing House, 1961

GENERAL

Walter Kolarz, *Books on Communism*, London, Ampersand, 1963

S. V. Utechin, *Everyman's Concise Encyclopaedia of Russia*, London, Dent, 1961

USSR: Questions and Answers, Moscow, Novosti Press Agency, 2nd edition, 1967. This agency, which specialises on information about the USSR for foreign countries, belongs to the Union of Soviet Journalists. The book contains a great deal of information but is unscrupulously propagandist

Herbert J. Ellison, *History of Russia*, New York, 1964

R. N. Taaffe and R. C. Kingsbury, *An Atlas of Soviet Affairs*, London, Methuen, 1965

PARTICULAR ASPECTS

Merle Fainsod, *How Russia is Ruled*, Oxford University Press, 1963 (684 large pages)

Leonard Schapiro, *The Government and Politics of the Soviet Union*, London, Hutchinson University Library, 1965 (191 small pages) (The above two books are by the leading American and British specialists respectively)

Abdurakhman Avtorkhanov, *The Communist Party Apparatus*, Chicago, Henry Regnery Co., 1966

Antony Buzek, *How the Communist Press Works*, London, Pall Mall Press, 1964

David and Vera Mace, *The Soviet Family*, London, Hutchinson, 1964

Emily Clark Brown, *Soviet Trade Unions and Labour Relations*, Harvard University Press, USA, 1966

Nigel Grant, *Soviet Education*, Penguin Books, 1964

Alec Nove and J. A. Newth, *The Soviet Middle East; a Communist Model for Development?*, London, Allen & Unwin, 1967

R. E. F. Smith, *How People Live in the USSR*, London, 1966 (geographical, for younger children)

Harrison E. Salisbury (ed.), *Anatomy of the Soviet Union*, London, Nelson, 1968 (comprehensive survey by various authors, including aspects of daily life)

George W. Simmonds (ed.), *Soviet Leaders*, New York, Thomas Y. Crowell, 1968 (biographies of 42 leaders in politics and other fields)

Leonid Vladimirov, *The Russians*, London, Pall Mall Press, 1968 (the best general account by a recent émigré)

William Taubman, *The View from Lenin Hills: Soviet Youth in Ferment*, London, Hamish Hamilton, 1968

George Feifer, *Justice in Moscow*, London, Bodley Head, 1964

Michael Bourdeaux, *Opium of the People*, London, Faber & Faber, 1965

Alec Nove, *The Soviet Economy*, London, Allen & Unwin, 1965

H. W. Morton, *Soviet Sport*, London, Collier-Macmillan, 1963

Laurens van der Post, *Journey into Russia*, London, Hogarth Press, 1964

Yuri Krotkov, *The Angry Exile*, London, Heinemann, 1967

Andrew Field (ed.), *Pages from Tarusa*, London, Chapman & Hall, 1965 (Translation of a volume of stories, poems and essays, mainly by young Soviet writers, which got past the censorship in 1961 without being 'socialist realist' and was immediately banned)

Thomas P. Whitney (translator and ed.), *The New Writing in Russia*, Ann Arbor, University of Michigan Press, 1964 (items by five Soviet authors published in the USSR in a recent period of relatively relaxed censorship, mostly in 1961–2)

C. P. Snow and Pamela Hansford Johnson (ed.), *Winter's Tales; Seven Stories from Modern Russia*, London, Macmillan, 1961

L. Labedz and M. Hayward, *On Trial; The Case of Sinyavsky (Tertz) and Daniel (Arzhak)*, London, Harvill Press, 1967

Andrei D. Sakharov, *Progress, Coexistence and Intellectual Freedom*, London, Deutsch, 1968 (a realistic analysis of Soviet and world problems by a leading Soviet scientist; not published in the USSR)

Greville Wynne, *The Man from Moscow*, London, Hutchinson, 1967, Arrow Books 1968 (authentic account of spying and prison conditions 1960–64)

A series of eight short and authoritative books on the USSR, edited by Robert Conquest, were published by the Bodley Head, London, in late 1967 and 1968. The titles are *Industrial Workers in the USSR, The Politics of Ideas in the USSR, Soviet Nationalities Policy in Practice, The Soviet Political System, Religion in the USSR, The Soviet Police System, Justice and the Legal System in the USSR, Agricultural Workers in the USSR*. Their method is to combine a large collection of facts on each topic, with full references, into a clear narrative of development since the revolution. The set is entitled 'Soviet Studies Series', but has no connection with the journal *Soviet Studies*

PERIODICALS ON THE USSR

Survey; a Journal of Soviet and East European Studies, London, quarterly, £2 per annum

Problems of Communism, Washington, bi-monthly, obtainable outside the USA from the US Information Service

Soviet Studies (including Information Supplement), University of Glasgow, quarterly, £3 per annum

The contributors to the above three journals are scholars. The first is best for descriptive material, the second is issued by the United States government and the third is academic

SOVIET PERIODICALS IN ENGLISH

Soviet Literature, a monthly issued by the Union of Soviet Writers. Contains new prose and poetry, criticism and features on the arts. The items are selected for foreign readers but the contents give some indication of current writing in the USSR. (Obtainable from Central Books, 37 Gray's Inn Road, London, W.C.1)

Sputnik, an illustrated monthly magazine obtainable from news-agents in Britain

Index

The numerals in **bold type** refer to the page on which illustrations appear

Watch factory, **36**
Water supplies, 54, 96, 125
Webb, Beatrice and Sidney, *Soviet Communism*, 178
Weddings, Palaces of, **183**
Whitney, T. P. (ed.), *New Writing in Russia*, 191
Woman Worker, 166
Women in farming, 57, 64, **67,** 78
  industry, 130, 136, **138**
  medicine, 138, 175
  professions, 138
  teaching, 171
  legislation concerning, 137
  magazines for, 166
Workers, auxiliary (MOP), 130
  dismissal of, 131
  grading of, 130
  manual, 129, 137
  non-manual, 129
  promotion of, 133–4

technical (ITR), 128, 129
  training, 133–4
Working class, incomes and living standards, 110
Working hours, 133
  idle time, 133
Works aristocracy and hierarchy, 128 ff.
Writers, 178, 192
  Union of Soviet, 119, 146, 178
Writing, free Soviet, published abroad, 179

Yesenin-Volpin, Alexander, 9, 10, 189
Yevtushenko, **177**
Young Communist League, 104, 105, 122, 126, 143, 145, 166, 175
Young Pioneers, 17, **48,** 174, 184

Zenkovsky, *History of Russian Philosophy*, 177
Zionism, 22
Zvenigorod, 73